COVERED CALL WRITING

Demystified:

Double-Digit Returns on Stocks in a Slower Growth Market for the Conservative Investor

Paul D. Kadavy

Arrow Publications

ARROW PUBLICATIONS

P.O. Box 19464
Fountain Hills, Arizona 85269-9464
E-mail address: arrowpublications@cox.net
Web site: www.arrowpublications.net

Manufactured in the United States of America
Library of Congress Control Number: 2001097592
ISBN 0-9715514-0-5
Cover Design: Real Image – Fountain Hills, Arizona

Although the author has extensively researched appropriate sources to ensure the accuracy and completeness of the information contained in this publication, the author and the publisher assume no responsibility for errors, inaccuracies, omissions, or any inconsistency herein. All of the characters in this book are fictitious. Any resemblance to actual persons, living or dead, is purely coincidental.

This publication is designed to provide accurate and authoritative information in regard to the subject matter covered. It is sold with the understanding that neither the author nor the publisher is engaged in rendering legal, tax, accounting, investment, or other professional services. No such advice is intended or implied.

All companies named in this publication have been included purely for purposes of illustration. No recommendation to buy, sell, or hold the common stocks, options or other securities of these companies, or any other company, is intended. Readers should use their own judgment. If advice or other expert assistance is required, the services of a competent professional person should be sought.

Trademark notice: Product or corporate names may be trademarks or registered trademarks, and are used only for identification and explanation, without intent to infringe.

COVERED CALL WRITING
DEMYSTIFIED

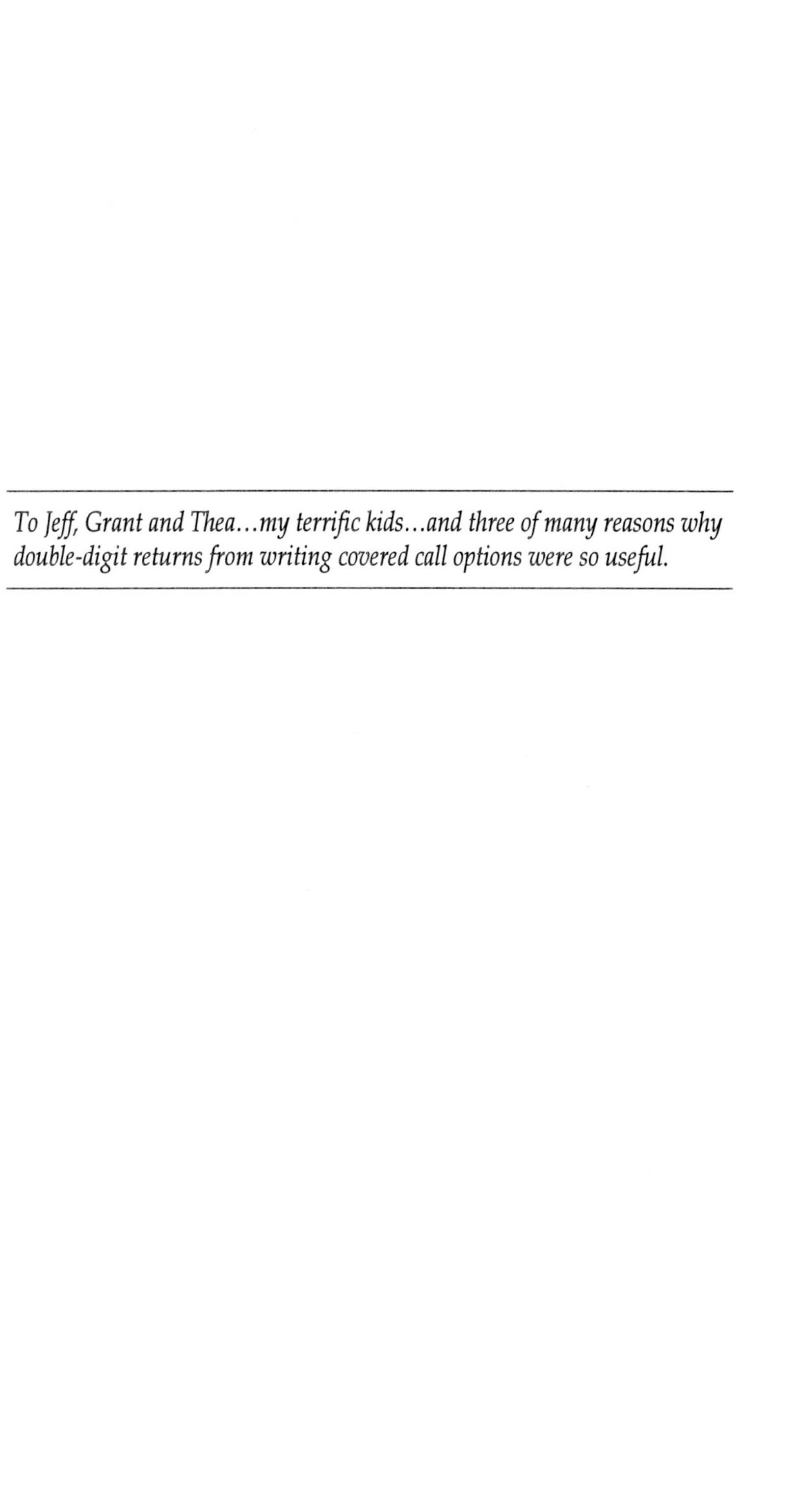

To Jeff, Grant and Thea…my terrific kids…and three of many reasons why double-digit returns from writing covered call options were so useful.

**NOTE REGARDING THE EXCEL FILES
INCLUDED WITH THIS BOOK
ON THE CD/ROM INSIDE THE BACK COVER:**

If the CD/ROM included with this book is damaged or if any of the file templates are corrupted, or if you are unable to use the files in this format, please send an e-mail to arrowpublications@cox.net. We will promptly provide you with the files by return e-mail.

CONTENTS

> Every day I get up and look through the Forbes list of the richest people in America. If I'm not there, I go to work.
>
> Robert Orben

Dear Reader/Investor:

"It takes money to make money."

This truism has likely been around since the creation of money itself. *Covered Call Writing Demystified* is designed for people who already have money…either quite a lot of it, or some of it with the ability to add to it on a regular basis. It is for those who want first to preserve it from the effects of inflation and also want to make it grow to support them and to add to their wealth while assuming an acceptable amount of risk commensurate with the return.

Keeping our money and making it grow may become more difficult than it has been in the past. Many investment experts and economists have been making public statements about investor expectations for the long-term future. They are suggesting that investors should not hope for anywhere near the level of investment returns from the stock market that they have come to expect over the past two decades. They believe that, at best, investors may realize from five-percent to seven-percent annual returns before taxes and inflation going forward.

If this prediction from such highly qualified experts is close to accurate, new ideas will be needed if stock market investors are to have any hope of achieving double-digit returns in the future.

Will the stock market only grow by five-percent to seven-percent annually, on average, for the next fifteen to twenty years as many experts are projecting?

Will stock investors still seek to achieve greater than five-percent to seven-percent annually on their investment assets?

If both of these questions are answered affirmatively, another important question needs to be answered: In this environment, what investment vehicles are capable of achieving greater than average stock market returns in the future? For most prudent investors, the possible choices are:

- **Tangible investments, gold and other precious metals** – Very unlikely to outperform, as these assets rise in value primarily in a high inflationary environment and in times of ongoing crisis. Economists are generally predicting low inflation for the future. And even in today's tense international environment that may cause short-term swings, the long-term outlook would not point to outperformance of such assets.

- **Bonds** – While there may be some additional capital appreciation potential in bonds should interest rates come down further, the coupon rate on bonds is already very low. They have appreciated very substantially in recent years. Bonds can provide an important fixed income component to a well-balanced investment portfolio, however, bonds do not outperform stocks over long periods of time.

- **Real estate** – Significant appreciation may potentially occur in well-selected real estate investments. Such investments are, however, generally quite illiquid. Investment advisors suggest only a small portion of investable assets should be placed into real estate investments.

- **Stock selection** – Some investors may feel that they can "beat the market" by diligent stock selection. This has proven to be illusory over long periods of time, even for professional portfolio managers with the very best track records.

- **Covered call writing** – Using standardized, exchange-traded options for covered call writing on common stocks, the combined return to the investor from potential capital appreciation, stock dividends and option premium income can result in double-digit yields...more predictably and conservatively than with common stocks alone. Covered call writing is a new subject for most individual investors and is misunderstood by many others.

The program outlined in *Covered Call Writing Demystified*, a combination of prudent ownership of common stocks coupled with writing covered call options on them, provides what may be one of the best opportunities to achieve double-digit investment returns in the future.

The investment strategy known as covered call writing involves the ownership or purchase of common stocks on which call option contracts are sold (written). By selling call option contracts on stock, the investor receives current income from option premiums, in addition to any dividends, and a defined amount of capital appreciation potential on the stock. This approach is more conservative than simply owning stocks. It can provide more stable, predictable, and higher investment returns than stock ownership alone in a slower growth stock market. *but not just slower mkts.*

This book may be the only title exclusively devoted to the subject of covered call option writing that presents the subject material in a manner easy for the reader to understand and with a personal investment program for implementation by the reader. Software templates for a personal computer using Microsoft® Excel are provided with the book to assist the user in formulating investment decisions on covered call writing opportunities, for tracking results and to assist with other financial planning decisions.

This book is written as a novel for easy readability. Yet its purpose is to serve as a hands-on, practical workbook for individuals who seek to achieve a consistent double-digit total return compounded annually on the common stock portion of their investment assets year after year.

No doubt one of your goals is to build wealth in anticipation of retirement someday, or perhaps you are already retired and are simply attempting to earn more than you currently spend to improve your standard of living. Also, rather than just leaving a will that says "Being of sound mind, I spent it all," you may wish to leave a legacy to family and charity. Consistently earning an above average real (after inflation) rate of return on your investments is critical to successfully achieving such financial goals.

Individuals with an investment portfolio of self-managed personal and retirement accounts are the primary intended audience for this book. These would typically be individuals who are finishing or have completed their strongest asset building years...people in their mid-fifties or older who have been accumulating assets for retirement or who have achieved their asset accumulation goals and are now retired.

Another audience consists of the many investors who have fewer investment assets, but are in a position to add substantially to them on a regular basis in the future. The growth of Exchange Traded Funds, and the increasing number of option investment products available in conjunction with them, provides this very large investor population with an opportunity to utilize the program outlined in this book. Such individuals would range in age from the twenties through mid fifties. The baby boom generation constitutes a huge portion of the higher-aged end of this profile group. These individuals are projected to substantially add to their investment asset wealth as they approach retirement and will inherit record amounts of assets in the near-term future.

Many people spend little time actively managing their investments. Such neglect leaves them open to the influence of advertising, suggestions from friends and relatives, or worse. It's no wonder so many investors end up on the wrong path. Yogi Berra's confusing directions, "When you come to a fork in the road, take it!" isn't far from reality for some.

This book will introduce a program most likely quite new to you. When implemented as suggested, it will help you find a new road and keep you firmly on it.

As a bank president, I was always amazed by how many customers would leave large sums in non-interest bearing checking accounts or very low-yield checking or savings accounts, without apparent concern for the paltry or non-existent returns that they were receiving. Such a passive approach to investing reminds me of an out-of-touch person who was asked whether he believed that there was widespread ignorance and apathy among the population. He responded, "I don't know and I don't care!"

People who place their money in bank certificates of deposit (CDs) or Treasury securities would love to get even a seven-percent rate today on their funds. Some have had an opportunity to earn as much or even more in the past. Now such a return on these investments is no longer even remotely possible in today's economic climate, and there does not seem to be much hope of achieving it anytime soon. Many people today are only earning four-percent or five-percent on their investment funds, or even less. Of course, we can assign some value to the fact that bank and savings and loan deposits are insured and Federal government securities are guaranteed.

Others who have been heavily invested in common stocks have achieved double-digit returns in some years, but have seen huge swings in their investment portfolios as they have taken big risks without fully understanding them...especially in the technology sector. Well-respected experts tell us it is extremely unlikely that those large returns of the past will be achievable in the future through traditional stock investing. Historically there has at least been some stability from the dividends shareholders received on their stocks. Now more and more companies pay no dividend. And for those that do, the return to the investor based upon the market value of their stock is pitifully low, often being no greater than a 1% to 1 ½% return.

Yet, achieving high rates of return always remains a fundamental goal for investors under any investment climate...if we can only determine how to do it. Let's take a look at the dramatic difference a higher return can make over time. For purposes of simplicity, we will assume that an investor has an initial investment of $100,000 in a Rollover IRA account. Therefore, there are no current taxes to pay on investment gains and income. The difference in the value of the account over many years can be staggering. Consider the implications if it were possible to achieve a fifteen-percent compounded annual return.

Rate:	6%	15%
Year:		
10	$179,085	$404,556
20	$320,714	$1,636,654
30	$574,349	$6,621,177

The program provided in this book to assist you in achieving double-digit compounded annual returns might be more conservative or more aggressive than your current investment approaches. Suffice it to say for now that the program involves more risk than placing your money in a bank, but less risk than simply being invested in the stock market.

Actually, a strong case can be made that leaving a substantial portion of your investments in lower return fixed income assets, such as CDs, savings accounts, bonds or mortgage investments, may in the long run be higher risk than the program presented here. The ongoing ravages of inflation continue to gnaw away at our collective net worth year after year, even at today's lower inflation rates. With only a three-percent annual inflation rate, the purchasing power of our money would decline by half in about twenty-four years. And, if we ever get back to the six-percent inflation range again, it would be cut in half about every twelve years. Never underestimate the ability of inflation to diminish our purchasing power over long periods of time.

By achieving a double-digit annualized return, an investor could expect to outpace inflation many times over. Most people would be able to add considerably to their net worth each year or could produce extra income to cope with rising expenses and improve their overall standard of living.

It is true that investments in some common stocks have yielded annualized returns, almost entirely from capital appreciation, of greater than fifteen-percent in some recent years. Yet a close examination would indicate that few have been able to achieve these results consistently over very long time periods (Warren Buffett excepted, of course). A large number of stocks have actually declined in value over the past few years. And the stocks that have previously performed so well, many in the high risk technology sector, are still selling at lofty prices by all historical standards, even after one of the most precipitous market corrections in history.

If you are currently a stock market or equity mutual fund investor who makes your own investment decisions, regardless of the size of your portfolio, and would like to add more stability and predictability to your investment returns and be afforded some protection in a down market, then this book is for you.

If you have typically kept your assets in bank deposits, are not happy with your investment returns, have considered going into the stock market, but are concerned about the risks, then this book is for you.

If you are interested in stock market investing, but your investment resources are limited, yet growing, this book is still for you. As diversification is important in all investment programs, note particularly the chapter on the new Exchange Traded Funds (ETFs) and how to use them in this program.

If you do not have the patience or desire to manage your own investment portfolio, this book is for your investment advisor or financial planner.

If you would be unable to sleep at night by having some of your money invested in the stock market, then this book may not be for you...but read and work through it anyway. You might change your mind and come to the conclusion that being out of the market also has its risks.

This book is for those who believe that long-term inflation is always a risk to overcome, but are concerned that the stock market alone may not provide the returns that it has in the past. It is for those of you who hope to still achieve a double-digit annual return on your investments despite the predictions of a slower growth market. If you are willing to take some risk to accomplish this, but not as much risk as just being in the stock market alone, then this book is for you.

By reading the story, following the numerous examples, and using the tools in this book, you will have a viable means of working towards this worthwhile objective.

* * * * *

A brief word regarding the call option writing examples in this book. Hypothetical company names have been used for individual stocks (e.g., "AAA," "BBB," "JJJ" and so on). These do, however, represent actual option trading opportunities for real companies based upon data obtained at the time the examples were created. The company names have been changed since information concerning real companies, such as price of securities, dividend rates, and other information, becomes out of date immediately after the slice of time from which it was taken. Fortunately the principles applied in the examples remain valid.

The reader should also be aware that brokerage commissions and other transaction costs have not been included in the investment calculations for the examples to simplify the subject matter presented. Such costs are discussed and would need to be considered in actual calculations. Provisions have been made to customize the software included with this book to fit the user's own commission schedule.

At the end of most of the chapters are exercises called "Practical Applications for Making Money." Many relate specifically to covered call option writing. Some are more general investment topics that may be of greater interest to readers who are less well acquainted with financial planning and the use of the Internet.

Prior to trading any option, an investor must receive a copy of *Characteristics and Risks of Standardized Options*. A copy may be obtained from the investor's broker or on the Internet at www.cboe.com.

Paul D. Kadavy

THE NEED FOR PREDICTABLE, BUT LARGE, INVESTMENT RETURNS

> A budget is just a method of worrying *before* you spend money, as well as *afterward.*
>
> Anonymous

After more than three decades of careful planning, it had almost become reality. Since his early twenties, Ernie Nuff had been preparing financially for the possibility that he might be able to swing early retirement when he turned age fifty-five. He was closing in on the goals he had set for himself. Many years ago a close friend had asked Ernie what he thought his net worth would have to be to retire early…most every person's dream. Being a banker, Ernie was savvy about such things, even though he was in the early stages of his career at that time. There was no standard rule of thumb to answer this question. It would depend on the individual and his or her circumstances, expectations, dreams, and no doubt a host of other factors that could develop and change over a period of many years. One of those other factors for Ernie was his marriage to Karen Welly Nuff, or Karie, as everyone called her. In addition to being a loving partner, through her job and her joint efforts with Ernie on their future plans she was a big contributor to their financial success as well.

The question Ernie's friend had asked got him thinking decades ago about what he really would need to accomplish his lofty goal. We won't go into detail about how Ernie figured it out, because the answers were a process unique to him and to Karie. Suffice it to say that they did it rationally, based upon a realistic expectation of what their expenses were back then and what they thought their expenses would be when Ernie would retire, considering their desired lifestyle at retirement. Other important factors included inflation expectations, investment returns they thought they could achieve, the degree of their willingness to take investment risk and their ability to save and make sacrifices to achieve their plan. All of this was quantified on paper. And, as the personal computer came into being, Ernie and Karie became more and more adept at putting their financial assumptions and projections into a computer spreadsheet program. Of course, the plan was updated on a regular and continuing basis.

When he first started planning, Ernie figured he would have to be a millionaire to have a shot at early retirement. It sounded impossible to someone in his early twenties, but he had a plan and he set out on the path to achieve it. As Ernie often said to his friends, "If you don't know where you're going, any road will take you there!" Ernie knew where they were going financially. Their road was the right road for them. Ernie and Karie's projections became more precise as their own experience and financial sophistication matured. Their projections included their house and other possessions and investment assets, consisting of their personal investments, his 401(K) plan, and his company pension, which he would plan to take in cash and place into a Rollover IRA so he could invest it himself.

Even after over thirty years of careful planning, it seemed like a miracle to Ernie and Karie that they were actually achieving their plan as the time approached for retirement.

Looking back over the years, they made note of what had made the biggest difference in allowing them to reach their financial goals. The diligence in their planning (the "road") was very important. Their willingness to sacrifice current spending desires over the years and stick to their plan had been critical too. But most important of all had been their long-term investments in common stocks, including the stock in the company Ernie worked for. As Ernie advanced at the bank, he continued to become more and more knowledgeable about stocks, bonds, and other financial investments. He knew that over long periods of time common stocks far outperformed other financial assets, and thus he saw their commitment to stocks as key to achieving their financial goal. It was true that Ernie and Karie had seen wide fluctuations in the value of their stocks over time, occasionally experiencing years in which stocks increased by over thirty-percent in value and other years in which they had declined by double-digits. But over many years it had all smoothed out. A good, solid return had been achieved and their goal was finally within sight.

But was it really that simple? All of the planning and investing that Ernie and Karie had done over these years helped them understand some of the new realities of a retirement life. First, they could not just put their money into fixed income investments like bank accounts, money market accounts or bonds and get the rate of return they would need to live on for the rest of their lives. They most likely had long lives ahead of them and still had a lot of expenses going forward. The mortgage had not yet been fully paid off, one of their children was still in college, and their other expenses were certainly going to feel the effects of future inflation over the thirty-plus years of their collective future life expectancies.

These expenses would be there year after year, even though some would drop out (e.g., college after graduation, the mortgage after it was fully paid). New expenses would come in to play as well though. A new car now and then, travel, whatever. Fixed income investments simply would not provide them with the income they needed to meet these expenses and inflationary increases. Besides, they didn't just want to meet expenses every year. They wanted a growing safety cushion, so that their worth would increase in value over future years. They had built into their planning an expectation of what they wanted to eventually leave to their three children and to their favorite charities.

Another thing they clearly understood was that they could not afford to experience the wide fluctuations in the stock market from year to year that would inevitably occur. While a nice cash cushion to meet a year or two of expenses could easily be maintained if they wished, a big drop in the market would not sit well with anyone who retired early and was reliant on investments for future survival and comfort. Ernie and Karie not only wanted to retire early and enjoy doing the things they never had time to do before. They wanted to be able to sleep well at night in the belief that it was all secure. Yet, they couldn't just shift to fixed income investments. Based on historical rates of return, they would have to continue a substantial participation in the stock market to have a chance of achieving the returns they needed, fluctuations or not.

Ernie and Karie were particularly lucky to be in a position to retire early in spite of rather unfortunate timing that was totally out of their control. As Ernie approached his fifty-fifth birthday, it was a time when the Dow Jones Industrial Average and the Standard & Poors 500 had experienced declines. The NASDAQ (the so-called "market of the future") was trying to recover from a precipitous decline of over seventy-percent.

Of course, the discussion here regarding Ernie and Karie's estate and their expenses have absolutely nothing specifically to do with you. But the planning process and the smoothing out of future earnings to meet future expenses has everything to do with you if you are retired or anticipate retiring in the future...and especially if you are like Ernie and Karie and want to retire early.

One more very important fact. Ernie and Karie decided that they needed to achieve a long-term return of ten-percent on their stock investments to meet expenses comfortably and to outpace inflation, whatever it might be in the future. They also wanted to see their net worth grow by two-percent compounded annually year after year for their own piece of mind and to continue to build the estate for their children and their charitable interests. From this, Ernie and Karie determined that the next, and final, piece of their long-term financial plan was the desire to achieve a consistent annual return on their stock investments...of twelve-percent.

Some people dream

of worthy accomplishments,

while others stay awake

and do them.

WARREN BUFFETT'S WARNING ABOUT FUTURE STOCK MARKET RETURNS

> If you can count your money, you don't have a billion dollars.
>
> J. Paul Getty

Ernie Nuff had spent his Monday evening in typical fashion…surfing the Internet on his laptop computer. Since establishing his online service a few years back, Ernie had become increasingly amazed at the volume of information available over the Internet for the asking…information that would otherwise have to be researched in a library or elsewhere. At the top of Ernie's list was investment research. He was knowledgeable about the world of investments from his job as a banker. Having used the Internet for some years, he knew what a valuable resource it could be, but that a person had to be cautious about the quality of the information obtained online. *Caveat emptor* obviously applied.

Ernie signed off of his computer and left his home office, looking for Karie. He found her in the family room where she was watching television.

"Karie, I was just doing some research on the Internet and I found something that bothers me a lot."

Karie looked up at him quizzically.

"I think you are familiar with Warren Buffett, the guy they call 'The Wizard of Omaha' or 'The Oracle of Omaha,'" Ernie said.

"Of course," Karie responded. "My Uncle Jim has owned stock in his company, Berkshire Hathaway, for quite a few years and has done very well with it. In fact, Uncle Jim suggested years ago that we invest in the company, if you recall."

"Oh, right. I'd forgotten that. It certainly would have been a good move," Ernie continued, a bit embarrassed that he had forgotten about Uncle Jim's excellent recommendation. "Well, anyway, I was using my favorite search engine, Google.com, as I often do to research investment information. I recently saw on the TV stock market channel, CNBC, that Berkshire Hathaway was buying another company and I was wondering what Warren Buffett is thinking about the stock market these days and where stock prices are headed."

"He usually doesn't comment much," Karie said. "In fact, Uncle Jim says that although Mr. Buffett's talks at his company's annual meetings are always very enlightening, and also entertaining, he doesn't get much into discussion about stock prices even then."

"I know that's been true in the past," Ernie agreed, "and that's why I was surprised to find this reference on Google.com to an article by a writer for *Fortune* magazine that was written just before the NASDAQ market started its huge decline. The author was quoting statements Buffett made about the stock market of the past and its prospects going forward. These unusual statements were made by Buffett to some of his friends and were written by the author and then reviewed by Buffett himself."

"What did Mr. Buffett have to say?" Karie inquired.

"Well, that's what is disturbing, because he said that the high performing stock markets of past years can't be duplicated going forward. In fact, it seems to me that he paints a pretty bleak picture. Here, let me read some of this to you," Ernie insisted. He shuffled the pages he had printed off of the Internet site and read Warren Buffett's words out loud:

> *Today, staring fixedly back at the road they just traveled, most investors have rosy expectations. I think it's very hard to come up with a persuasive case that equities will over the next 17 years perform anything like--anything like--they've performed in the past 17. If I had to pick the most probable return, from appreciation and dividends combined, that investors in aggregate--repeat, aggregate--would earn in a world of constant interest rates, 2% inflation, and those ever hurtful frictional costs, it would be 6%. If you strip out the inflation component from this nominal return (which you would need to do however inflation fluctuates), that's 4% in real terms. And if 4% is wrong, I believe that the percentage is just as likely to be less as more.* [1]

"That's exactly what he said. And I found that Mr. Buffett also warned the shareholders of his company, Berkshire Hathaway, at its annual meeting that investors should expect, he said, 'returns from equities that are dramatically less than most investors have either experienced in the past

---

[1] Carol Loomis, "Mr. Buffett on the Stock Market," *Fortune* (Vol. 140, No. 10, Special Issue, November 22, 1999): 212.

or expect in the future.' [2] That's what Buffett said to the stockholders of his own company, Karie. His associate, Vice Chairman Charlie Munger was also quoted as saying that six-percent to seven-percent would be a reasonable expectation of annual stock market growth for the next ten to twenty years. [3] And in the comments to the shareholders in their written annual report, Buffett said 'Our restrained enthusiasm for these securities (referring to Berkshire Hathaway's stock holdings) is matched by decidedly lukewarm feelings about the prospects for stocks in general over the next decade or so.'" [4]

"It's really ironic that you should bring this up right now, Ernie. I was watching *Moneyline* on CNN awhile back. I was struck by an interview Lou Dobbs did on the program with Douglas Cliggott, who is the Chief Equity Strategist for J.P. Morgan Securities. Dobbs asked him what kind of returns investors in the stock market should expect in the future. Cliggott answered, 'I think something like five-percent, six-percent is the type of return that we should plan on.' [5] I didn't think much of it back then, but it sounds like he and Mr. Buffett pretty much agree on the fact that things won't be quite so easy going forward. We should definitely pay

---

[2] Comment made by Warren Buffett, Chairman of the Board of Berkshire Hathaway, Inc., at its annual shareholders meeting held April, 2001 in Omaha, Nebraska.

[3] Comment made by Charlie Munger, Vice Chairman of Berkshire Hathaway, Inc., at its annual shareholders meeting held April, 2001 in Omaha, Nebraska.

[4] "Chairman's Letter, "Berkshire Hathaway 2001 Annual Report: 15.

[5] Interview with Douglas Cliggott, Chief Equity Strategist for J.P. Morgan Securities, by Lou Dobbs, *Moneyline*, CNN, August 20, 2001.

attention to what they are saying," Karie said with a look of concern on her face.

"I certainly buy into that," Ernie agreed. "I know our planning shows we need a much larger overall return than five-percent or six-percent or seven- percent if we are going to be able to retire later this year when I turn fifty-five."

"What do you think we should do?" Karie asked.

Ernie pondered deeply for a moment and then replied emphatically, "Tomorrow at work I'm going to spend some time with The Guru."

PRACTICAL APPLICATIONS FOR MAKING MONEY

One of the best ways to find information about investments on the Internet is through a "search engine." By placing one or more key words into a search engine it will compile huge indexes of Web sites hopefully containing the information about the subject you are seeking. For those who are already familiar with search engines, you know that you can access a wealth of information on virtually any subject (both reliable and unreliable), including the world of investments.

Some of the more popular search engines are the following:

- www.google.com
- www.alltheweb.com
- www.altavista.com
- www.dogpile.com
- www.yahoo.com
- www.hotbot.com
- www.excite.com
- www.teoma.com
- www.go.com
- www.webcrawler.com
- www.metacrawler.com

If you are not familiar with the use of search engines, try going to www.google.com and type in "Berkshire Hathaway." Google will provide a list of Web sites from which you can choose. Click on the first link given (www.berkshirehathaway.com). This will take you to that company's Web site. Click on the link that says "Annual Reports – 1995 –2000." Next click on "2000 Annual Report." Then click on "2000 Annual Report PDF Version." (Note: if you do not have the Adobe Acrobat program on your computer, click first on the word "Adobe" above on the Web page. When the report comes up, scroll to the sixth paragraph on page three of the report and you will see the statement by Warren Buffett that is quoted by footnote four in Chapter 2 of this book.)

This is just one example of how a search engine can be used. Try it out by typing in some of your favorite investment terms or subjects to see where it will take you. Also, you might want to check out the following sites:

http://money.cnn.com/markets/us_markets.html

and

http://money.cnn.com/markets/morning_call/

After the markets close each day, and Sunday evenings, you can see how the markets' futures contracts (Globex) are trading around the world. A positive or negative futures market may give an indication of whether the corresponding stock markets will open positively or negatively the next day.

WHY WILL MARKET GROWTH LIKELY BE SLOWER IN THE FUTURE?

There are many financial experts who believe that stock market returns in the future will be significantly less than they have been in the past. They offer several themes to support their conclusions:

- Despite market corrections in the major averages...the Dow Jones Industrial Average, the Standard & Poors 500, and most especially the NASDAQ...stocks are still selling at heftier prices now than even a historical midpoint of a range of values for these averages.

- A bubble was created in the Internet and telecommunications sectors through unprecedented access by startup companies to the capital markets, resulting in unsustainable levels of capital spending. This has been unwinding for some time as the bubble burst. Many believe that such a bursting has long-term implications that will slow future economic growth and affect other industries as well.

- Corporate profits would have to grow at an abnormally high rate in the future as a percentage of Gross Domestic Product (national output) to support much higher stock prices. Since this is very unlikely, the relatively high level of current stock prices will increase more slowly as corporate earnings growth works to catch up and bring about more normal stock price averages in the future.

- Interest rates are now at lows not seen since the Kennedy Administration in the 1960s. Inflation is very low. Both of these factors are certainly strong supporters of relatively high stock prices. Yet to support significantly higher stock prices, both interest rates and inflation would need to decline even more. The problem is that there is almost no additional room for either to decline further.

These are the primary schools of thought regarding why stock prices are highly likely to grow at a slower pace in the future than they have in the past. Investors would be well served by watching these factors.

For owners of stocks, writing covered call options on them may be the best opportunity to achieve double-digit returns in this projected future.

THE INVESTOR/BANKER AND THE GURU MEET

A bank is a place where they lend you an umbrella in fair weather and ask for it back when it begins to rain.

Robert Frost

The bank where Ernie worked was a large one, and it had its own trust department. Max Cashman headed the Investment Division for the bank's trust department, having been in that position for many years. Out of respect for Max's track record in stock investing for the trust department's client base, he had come to be referred to as "The Guru" by bank staff, customers, and even some of his peers in the investment business. Ernie trusted Max's judgment completely. He knew that Max would be just the person to help sort out how to plan the management of his and Karie's investments to meet their retirement income and asset growth needs...if anyone could do it in a slower growth stock market climate.

Ernie called Max's assistant and made an appointment with him for that afternoon at the end of work.

When Ernie arrived, Max was busily sorting through investment reports and the results of the day's stock market activity. "How'd the market do today?" Ernie asked for starters.

"Oh, hi, Ernie," The Guru replied somewhat distractedly, placing his stacks of papers in neat piles to the side of his rather prodigious desk. "The NASDAQ faltered and it took the Dow down with it again!" Max answered. "It's going to take some time to work ourselves through this…and going forward it's not going to be as easy to make money in the market as it's been in the past, Ernie."

"Yeah," Ernie responded somewhat dejectedly. "That's kind of what I've been hearing. Sounds like all of you gurus are in agreement about that."

THE FUTURE ISN'T WHAT IT USED TO BE

"In fact," Max continued, "I heard Sir John Templeton, the pioneer in the mutual fund business and creator of the Templeton Funds, make a startling statement on CNBC. He said that over the next century you should expect your share prices to average an annual return of six-percent. He also said he thinks that over the next five or ten years we'll be lucky to come out even on share prices." [6]

Max had more. "Then Barton Biggs, chairman of Morgan Stanley Investment Management, commented about the performance of the markets here compared with Europe and other markets. He said that he expects the U.S. 'could be the worst big market in the world for a half-decade.' [7] And to cap it off, John Bollinger, the widely known technical analyst and creator of the 'Bollinger Bands', who appears regularly on CNBC, said 'The Dow has gone absolutely nowhere for

---

[6] Interview with Sir John Templeton, creator of the Templeton Funds, by Consuelo Mack, *Business Center*, CNBC, October 1, 2001.

[7] Andy Serwer, "Less Growling from this Bear," *Fortune* (Vol. 144, No. 8, October 29, 2001): 191

three, coming on four years now. I think it will last maybe for another ten years.'" [8]

"Pretty depressing," Ernie stated glumly.

"So, to what do I owe the pleasure of this visit today?" Max asked with a smile.

"Well, Max, we've known each other for a long time," said Ernie. "Over the years you and I have both said that we would like to be in a position to take early retirement if we could afford to do it with confidence. As you know, I'll be fifty-five years old in just a few months, and it looks like I might still have a shot at it, even with the declines we've had in the stock markets. Karie and I are on track to meet our goals, so now it's just a matter of making the decision."

"That's fantastic. Congratulations!" Max replied, reaching over to pat Ernie on the back. "I've heard that nobody on his deathbed ever said 'I wish I'd spent more time at the office.' Sounds like you've got that one solved! Don't forget though, Ernie, they say that old bankers never die, they just lose their interest!"

Ernie managed to crack a smile.

"But you've got a bit of a worried look on your face," Max noted. "What's on your mind?"

"Well," Ernie continued, wringing his hands a bit as he talked, "making a final decision on retirement is a bit scary. A person wants to be sure of doing the right thing. Time goes so fast, and inside every older person is a younger person wondering what the heck happened, if you know what I mean!

"You just hit the nail on the head a minute ago, Max. Smart investment people are saying that for many years to come we aren't going to be able to expect the large returns of

---

[8] Interview with John Bollinger by William Griffith, CNBC, October 29, 2001.

the past from common stocks. We've relied on that to help us meet our financial goals up to now, and it's worked pretty well," Ernie said proudly. "But now that we're at the brink, Karie and I went through our plan for retirement…you know, projecting current and future expenses, figuring in inflation and taxes, and how to continue to build assets to leave to the kids and charities we are interested in."

"Sounds like you are still the good planners that you always were," Max complimented.

"Planning isn't the problem, Max. We would like a fairly steady and predictable twelve-percent return on the stock portion of our investments year after year to be really comfortable that we are doing the right thing by taking early retirement. Obviously the safety net of income from our jobs won't be there any longer. And I know that once Karie and I start doing the things we hope to do we would never want to go back to a full-time job again…as much as I have liked working at the bank," Ernie said with complete seriousness.

"Well, we sure all got hooked on those huge stock market returns for so many years," Max admitted. "And with the markets, particularly the NASDAQ, down so significantly now, I'm guessing that a lot of people out there are changing their plans. You are very fortunate to still be in a position to even consider going ahead with early retirement."

Ernie nodded his head vigorously in agreement.

"As you know, I'm two years younger than you, Ernie," Max said, "but as you said, you and I have similar plans. The bank has been good to us financially, and we've been very fortunate that the company's stock has held up quite well under some pretty adverse market conditions. Frankly, I'm still on track too for early retirement when I turn fifty-five, so I'll be facing the same important problem you are confronted with now. I think it's very true that we can't expect stock market returns to be nearly as good as the past. Fortunately, I have a way to help reach the solution to that dilemma and I'd be happy to share it with you. It's so often unknown or misunderstood by investors that some think of it as a 'secret'... although it isn't a secret at all, just something new for many investors, even though it's been around since 1973."

"Really?" Ernie responded, immediately encouraged. Ernie thought that he should have known The Guru would have the answer, but somehow he expected a solution to the problem to be either non-existent or very difficult to deal with. "Well, that's why I'm here, Mr. Guru!"

Max blushed, as he always did when someone called him by that name, although there was no question in anyone's mind that he deserved the distinguished title that had been informally conferred upon him.

Max continued. "Before we talk about how it's done though, Ernie, we need to take a hard look at your specific investment situation now and your future plans. After that I'll share the complete program with you."

"Fair enough!" responded Ernie.

Ernie spent the next half-hour or so telling Max everything about his and Karie's current financial situation and what their needs and expectations were for retirement.

When he was finished, Max again congratulated Ernie on the great job that he and Karie had done in building their estate and achieving their investment goals. Ernie beamed, as hearing such words of praise from The Guru himself was indeed a high compliment.

"You've got two initial situations you have to deal with, Ernie, for you to be comfortable about early retirement," Max announced. "First, you will need to continue to have substantial exposure to common stocks in your investment portfolio going forward. The reason is very simple, and you are already aware of it because you brought the subject up yourself a minute ago. You can't achieve the returns you need by investing in fixed income producing assets alone. The other situation is that you will need to diversify your stock investments more broadly in anticipation of early retirement. Our company stock has served you very well over the years, but you are far over-concentrated in it."

Ernie smiled and nodded in complete agreement.

"From what you have just told me, some of the mutual funds and individual stocks you and Karie have acquired have done well and could be suitable for continued holding into retirement. Others may need some work," Max suggested as Ernie listened intently.

"To implement the investment program we will be discussing, there are two different paths that an investor can take...or a combination of both. One would be to own a portfolio of individual common stocks, sufficiently diversified to reduce overall risk. The second path would be to own a relatively new investment security, called an Exchange Traded Fund. It's traded like a stock, but in some ways is like a mutual fund and in some ways is different, because it can give you a lot more flexibility. The purpose of both of these paths is to assure good diversification. You can follow either of the paths, or a combination of the two of them. The first path, individual stocks, works well for investors who have sizeable portfolios. The second path also works well in large portfolios, but is ideal for investors with smaller investment assets."

Ernie thought about what Max had just said. "I'd be interested in learning more about this new kind of investment, Max, but I wouldn't want to give up owning individual stocks. I enjoy that and like to do some of my own research before making investment decisions."

"That's fine," Max countered. "We'll base our discussion around individual stock ownership. Later I'll tell you more about this new investment security too, because the program we will be discussing works exactly the same with it as it does with individual stocks.

"I think doing your own investment research is admirable, Ernie," Max continued. "But that's a big job, and any investor who is relying on investments to fund his retirement needs help with that.

"In fact, Ernie, I strongly suggest that you subscribe to an investment advisory service soon to get started with investment ideas on individual stocks for your retirement, and continue with such a service throughout your retirement. I will tell you now that owning mutual funds doesn't fit with the program I will be sharing with you. The new investment security I mentioned that has characteristics similar to mutual funds would work in their place, however. So if you decide to follow my program fully, you would need to liquidate your mutual funds, or keep some of them knowing that you wouldn't be able to use the program with them. You could use the money from the funds you sold to buy more individual common stocks, possibly some of these new investment securities, maybe some bonds, and to keep a nice reserve of cash at whatever level you are comfortable. I doubt that you want to spend all of your time in retirement researching excruciating details about stocks before you decide what to buy. A solid performing investment service will give you a firm foundation for stock selections...although I'm a strong advocate of personal research too."

"Are you suggesting that I should hire you to manage our investments?" Ernie said with a smile.

"Not at all," Max replied in surprise. "We do a good job for our clients here, Ernie, but I'm not by any means suggesting that you turn over your assets to me or anyone for active management unless that's something you would really prefer to do. It certainly isn't true of everyone, but you are knowledgeable enough to use a good investment service yourself to pick individual stocks and then use the program we will be discussing to get you the returns you need. It will work well for you, and you will save a lot of money compared to what you would pay if you hired us or someone else to do it for you."

Ernie appeared to be a bit puzzled, but was still listening to every word.

"Just hang in there with me for now, Ernie, and it will start to make more sense as we go on," Max stated. "What you need are solid portfolio suggestions for you to consider, do a little bit of research on over the Internet, and make sound decisions on what to buy, OK?"

"Yes," Ernie responded, "but even if I use a good service to get portfolio suggestions for commons stocks, that still leaves me with the exposure to big up and down swings in market prices. I need to avoid that if I'm going to be able to sleep at night when I retire. And then there's this slow growth stock market..."

"Patience, my good man!" Max insisted. "That's where my program comes in. But we won't have enough time to get into that today. In fact, if you are really serious about this, it will take several sessions together."

"Thanks, Max," Ernie replied. "I really appreciate your willingness to spend that much time with me. I wouldn't ask it of you if it weren't so important to our future."

"My pleasure, Ernie," Max countered. "But now let me give you a couple of my beliefs on stock selection. First, when you retire you need to avoid stocks that are highly speculative. For example, even though the Internet continues to grow and will no doubt be very viable for the future, we've seen many of the Internet stocks go down over the past year by as much as fifty-percent to ninety five-percent, and in some cases they've gone bankrupt. I just read in the paper yesterday that the number of 'dot com' companies that have gone out of business so far is headed toward one thousand, and many more are expected to do the same. You don't need that kind of agony in your retirement. At the same time, I'm not suggesting that you only buy stodgy stocks in fully mature industries that don't have much future growth opportunity in them either. You need some balance and diversification within your stock portfolio, but with the objective that your stocks, coupled with my program, will be structured to provide you with a more stable income to help you get to your twelve-percent goal each year for a long period of time. In other words, you aren't speculating for huge gains, you are investing to achieve a continuation of your plan, but in a different mode now. Does that make sense?" Max asked.

"It sure does, Max," Ernie agreed resoundly. "I can't wait to hear how your program fits into to all this. But I'll wait…until next time," Ernie said with a grin.

"You could get a lot of excellent investment ideas just through published information from many of the major bank trust departments. I know we publish a booklet each quarter that lists the largest holdings in our commingled funds…kind of like mutual funds, but for our trust customers. As you probably know, we have a variety of funds, some of them are more conservative and some more growth oriented. The objective of each of the funds is described in our booklet along with the top holdings. I'm sure that many if not all of the major trust departments publish such a booklet for their clients. It may be possible for a person to stop by and pick up one of these on request. Just a thought.

"You could do the same thing even more easily with the best performing mutual funds in the country. With a little research on the Internet or in the library, you could find out which mutual funds have objectives to buy the kind of stocks that would be suitable individual stocks for your retirement. Some mutual funds' Web sites even allow you to download their prospectus, and that would give you information about their objectives and key holdings.

"In fact, you can start by looking at your own current mutual funds. You must have literature on them that tells what the funds' objectives are and the stocks they hold, don't you?"

"Sure do," Ernie replied.

"What I'm suggesting, Ernie, is that such sources of ideas are as good or better than listening to the hodgepodge of ideas that come somewhat indiscriminately from thousands of sources over the Internet. This would be focused, and you could be sure that the stocks contained in these portfolios have objectives that would be consistent with your own."

What Max was saying did make sense to Ernie. Even though he didn't know the "secret" yet, if he was going to get out of mutual funds and even more into individual stocks, it made sense that a mutual fund or trust department fund with a similar objective to his own would contain many of the individual stocks that he might be interested in researching and perhaps buying.

INVESTMENT ADVISORY SERVICES

"Let me toss this out for your consideration, Ernie. What I've just suggested to you up to now is free information, but it's only a starting point. You need to take those ideas and run them through a filter of sorts…another source, to make sure they are really right for you. That's the investment advisory service I brought up.

"There are many good investment advisory services, Ernie, but I'm going to suggest two that I'm familiar with. There may be others you wish to consider," Max pointed out.

"I'd suggest you consider a subscription to Zacks Investment Research on the Internet. It's simple to set up, and you can take all of the stock ideas you come across and run it through Zacks to see how they rank them.

"Zacks has served institutional and individual investors since 1978. They organize and evaluate the research produced by U.S. brokerage firms and provide information based upon earnings expectations from analysts. Zacks focuses on the future earnings of companies, which is what ultimately drives their stock prices. Their research and information applies to both value and growth stocks. Also, they provide a useful reference on an ongoing basis to the best large stocks that many of the country's top brokerage firms are recommending. This is called the 'Brokerage Firm Buy List.' It would be a useful resource just by itself in selecting ideas for your own portfolio. This is a group of stocks that are currently appearing on the recommended lists of at least three of the top brokerage firms and are generally some of the best large capitalization stocks to own for the long-term. This list and a lot of other information is available for free by going to the www.zacks.com Web site.

"A key feature of the Zacks paid service is their 'Timely Buys' recommendations…stocks that they rank for short-term outperformance of the market, although often these stocks are more volatile than those in the 'Brokerage Firm Buy List.' There is also a section titled 'Education' that helps newer investors and assists subscribers in how to best use the service. Of course you can also get hard copy information and talk on the phone to their representatives as well."

"How do you sign up for this and how much is the subscription?" Ernie asked, always cost conscious.

"I wouldn't say it's cheap," Max admitted. "But, I think it's worth it if you use it right, and it can form the cornerstone of your stock selections. The current price is $199 for one year, or you can sign up for three years and pay $399. To register for a free trial of the paid subscription you need to go to the www.zacksadvisor.com Web site. You can try all of the features you will eventually get, so you are fully trained on it before you pay anything. You use the Internet a lot already, don't you?"

"You bet," Ernie answered quickly.

"Good!" Max responded equally as quickly. "The Internet will be the backbone of the investment research and trading that we will discuss. Anyone can do it, and using it can save a lot of money."

(Reader/Investor: If you do not have a computer or use the Internet, the resources in this book can be utilized without either of them by using the manual worksheets and instructions provided.)

"What are some of the stocks listed on the Zacks 'Brokerage Firm Buy List'?" Ernie wanted to know.

Max pulled a page out of a file folder in his desk and read off these names: "ADC Telecommunications, Alcoa, American Home Products, American International Group, Amgen, AOL/Time Warner, Applied Materials, Baxter International, Best Buy, Cisco Systems, Citigroup, Clear Channel, Dell Computer, El Paso Corp., Electronic Data Systems, Fannie Mae, Freddie Mac, General Electric, Home Depot, IBM, Intel, Johnson & Johnson, Kohls Corp., Metlife Inc., Medtronic, Mellon Financial, Microsoft, Motorola, Nokia, Pfizer, Target, Texas Instruments, Tyco International, Viacom and Wells Fargo. Of course, names change from time to time as brokerage company recommendations change."

"Impressive companies," Ernie admitted.

"I'll mention another investment service you might also want to look into…The Value Line Investment Survey. You can have an initial subscription for ten weeks for only $55. This gives you hard copy reports on about 1,700 individual stocks in more than ninety industries that are regularly updated. Or you can get the service online instead of hard copy. In any event, start out by going to the www.valueline.com Web site.

"They describe the service as a unique source of financial information designed to help investors make informed investment decisions that fit their individual goals and levels of risk. They consider themselves 'the most trusted and prestigious name in the investment field.' Value Line ranks each of these stocks from 1 through 5, and suggests that you pick from the top two categories in formulating and maintaining your portfolio. According to them, these top two ranking categories have significantly outperformed the overall markets over time.

"There's a wealth of information about these companies in their reports. One of the things I like about it is that it gives the average annual **'price/earnings'** ratio currently and over past years. You can get some idea of where the current P/E ratio stands in relation to the past, which is one measure to help determine whether the stock is overvalued or undervalued compared with its historic range.

"OK, Ernie…a little test before we close for today. What's the definition of P/E ratio?" Max asked.

Ernie reflected momentarily and then spoke. "The price/earnings ratio is figured by taking the current price of the stock and dividing it by the earnings per share. So, if a stock is selling for $30 per share and its earnings are $2 per share, it has a P/E ratio of 15. Usually you would use the past 12 months actual results, but sometimes people look at the projected earnings for the next twelve months to determine the expected P/E ratio looking forward," Ernie blurted out.

"Excellent, Ernie!" This is going to be easy work for you. Of course, there was a joke going around the investment community that the P/E ratio is the percentage of investors wetting their pants as the NASDAQ kept crashing!"

Ernie let out a hearty laugh.

"I often recommend that people get the book *The Wall Street Journal Guide To Understanding Money & Investing* if they need to develop an understanding of the fundamentals. But I can tell by the way you answered that question and the planning and successful investing you've done over the years that you already know what's needed," Max complimented.

"Well, thanks, Max," Ernie said gratefully. "For the advisory service, would you recommend Zacks or Value Line for us?"

"As important as this is, Ernie, I would suggest you try the introduction to both and see what they can do for you. You can use the initial Value Line hard copy information for quite awhile before you would need to buy the full subscription. By then you may have gotten what you need out of it in terms of an education, and then stick with Zacks. Try them both and see which works for you. Also, if you like Value Line, many libraries maintain an updated subscription to the service that you can use for free."

"I'll check them out, Max," Ernie responded eagerly.

"Well, I don't know about you, Ernie, but it's been a pretty long day for me. How about if we get together again on Friday? That will give you some time to take a look at the Zacks and Value Line Web sites. And on Friday, we'll start our discussion about how you might get that twelve-percent annual return you and Karie say you need to make things work. Fair enough?" Max asked.

"You bet!" Ernie responded. "I really appreciate your time today, Max. I can't wait to find out how this is going to work...but, thanks to you, I'm feeling a lot of confidence about it already."

"You're welcome, Ernie. And I'll leave you with an intriguing notion to think about between now and Friday. The investment ideas we are going to be discussing work best of all in a flat to slowly rising stock market!" Max said.

Ernie felt like he was walking a few inches off of the floor when he left Max's office. How in the world could there be a way to possibly achieve their twelve-percent return in a market that was flat or slowly rising? But that's what Max had suggested...and that was exactly the kind of market Warren Buffett, Sir John Templeton and other experts were projecting for many years to come.

PRACTICAL APPLICATIONS FOR MAKING MONEY

THE RULE OF 20

Is the market undervalued, fairly valued, or overvalued at this time? No one ever knows with any certainty, but one rule of thumb can be calculated by subtracting the annualized rate of consumer inflation (CPI) from 20. The theory is that the resulting figure represents about what the present price/earnings (P/E) ratio should be if the market is fairly valued. Information about the CPI is widely available on television and in newspapers. It can also be readily found by going to the Department of Labor's site on the Internet, http://stats.bls.gov/. On their main page you will find reference to the CPI. Just click on the link and you will see current information about the CPI. Plug their CPI number into the formula below and make the computation for the 'expected P/E ratio':

	Current Annualized	Expected
	Rate of inflation (CPI)	P/E Ratio
20 minus	______________________	= ______________________

This may only be marginally helpful, as the P/E ratio of major indexes has often been above 20 in recent years. There is a direct correlation between the level of short-term interest rates and P/E ratios. As short-term interest rates decline, P/E ratios tend to increase. Therefore, if P/E ratios are to be sustained above 20 for the market, short-term interest rates must be very low. Correspondingly, the CPI must also be very low, with the prospect of inflation being almost insignificant.

One measure would be to take the expected P/E ratio figure and compare it with the current P/E ratio of a broad market index such as the S&P 500, the Dow Jones Industrial Average, or the Wilshire 5000. The P/E ratios of these broad indexes are available from time to time on CNBC TV, financial and local daily newspapers, and on various Web sites on the Internet. For example, the P/E ratio for the Standard & Poors (S&P) 500 can be obtained by going to the Web site www.standardandpoors.com.

Complete and compare the following:

Expected P/E Ratio	P/E Ratio of S&P 500	P/E Ratio of DJII	P/E Ratio of Wilshire 5000
________	________	________	________

Based on this information, at what level is the market trading relative to the 'Rule of 20' expectations? If the actual P/E ratios for the S&P, Dow Jones Industrial Average and the Wilshire 5000 are well above the expected ratio, the market *may* be overvalued. Conversely, if the actual P/E ratios are below the expected level, the market *may* be undervalued.

This is only a guide, or rule of thumb. Additional research from other sources should be conducted to determine if this is a good time to commit new funds to the market or whether a cautious posture is more appropriate. Keep in mind that during periods of economic decline, earnings may be reduced considerably. Price earnings ratios therefore increase if earnings drop faster than a decline in stock prices. Since the stock market usually rises prior to an economic recovery, P/E ratios can actually rise before earnings recover. Therefore, this rule of thumb likely works best during stable economic times.

INVESTMENT ADVISORY SERVICES

If you have Internet access, go to www.valueline.com and www.zacks.com to see what is available on these sites. Find the "Brokerage Firm Buy List" on Zacks' site and view the stocks that are currently included. Make a list of the information that would be useful to you from a trial subscription to one or both of these services or from other investment advisory services.

Things turn out the best

for the people

who make the best

of the way things turn out.

John Wooden

4

SOME STARTLING BENEFITS

> Don't go around saying the world owes you a living. The world owes you nothing. It was here first.
>
> Unknown

Following the Monday meeting with The Guru, Ernie hurried home to discuss everything with Karie that Max had told him. Karie was equally excited about the possibility that Max's "secret" could help them get the twelve-percent return they wanted in order to retire. In fact, Karie was so interested in hearing more that she asked Ernie if she could join him at the next meeting with Max on Friday. Ernie was pleased with this, as they were full and equal partners in the retirement venture they were soon hoping to undertake.

The time between the Monday meeting and the next scheduled meeting on Friday seemed to drag on forever for Ernie. He felt very hopeful about where things were headed after the first meeting and couldn't wait for more information to help them transform their dream into reality.

Ernie had taken the opportunity between meetings to check out the Zacks Advisor and Value Line Web sites. As someone already knowledgeable about stocks and markets in general, Ernie understood how to take advantage of these services. He noted too that the tutorial information they both supplied online and in written form would also be highly instructive to those who are novices at investing. He felt that these services could be of great use to him and Karie in making individual stock selection decisions. He particularly liked the fact that both services made specific recommendations from which to choose, depending on an investor's risk tolerance profile, with the ability to be more conservative or aggressive as desired by the individual. He also liked the ability to develop ideas on their own and get an opinion and additional research from these services. As a result, Ernie and Karie took Max's recommendation and signed up for the free trial offer from Zacks and the trial subscription to Value Line. They were ready to move forward.

Friday afternoon finally arrived. Karie stopped by Ernie's desk, and together they went to see Max, who was in good spirits that day, as the stock markets had more than made up the lost ground earlier in the week.

After mutual greetings, and expressions from Max about how pleased he was to have Karie join them, Max started out by summarizing.

ERNIE'S AND KARIE'S INVESTMENT GOALS

"Ernie and Karie, if I understood correctly from my visit with Ernie earlier this week, given your plan to retire in the next few months, your goals going forward would be to adopt a lifetime investment methodology that will accomplish the following:

- Provide a return that will regularly outpace the cost of living (consumer inflation) by a wide margin.

- Provide a reasonably consistent twelve-percent compounded annual return on your stock investments and perhaps higher returns if you were in a position to assume commensurately higher risk on a portion of your assets.

- Provide a more stable and conservative approach than investing only in individual stocks.

- Result in easy administration of the investment process so you have plenty of time to enjoy other things in your retirement.

"Does that accurately summarize what you are looking for?" Max asked them both.

"Yes," Karie spoke for both of them. "Do you think we can do that?"

"I think the program I am going to suggest to you will work beautifully to help you achieve your goals. And I think you will have a lot of fun making it happen, " Max added.

Karie interrupted. "And Ernie said you had told him last time that your 'secret' actually works best in a flat to slowly rising market, right? I just don't understand how we can meet our goals if we have the kind of market Warren Buffet is suggesting we will have...what did he say, maybe an average of only six-percent or seven-percent annually over the next seventeen years!"

"First, I don't think of my program as a 'secret,' Karie, because it is widely available to anyone who wants to use it that knows how. It seems to be a secret because there has not been a resource available focused on its unique use that is clearly understandable and capable of implementation by most investors. But that's the purpose of the program we will be discussing together.

THE BENEFITS OF MAX'S PROGRAM

"To respond to your concern…not only will you have an opportunity to achieve your investment return goal in a slower growth stock market," Max confirmed, "but there are some other real plusses in this program that I want to tell you about to initiate our discussion." Max was set to really surprise them now.

"What would you say if I told you that the investment program I'm about to share with you would also do the following things for you?" Max picked up a sheet of paper and referred to it:

- When you use this investment program, your stock investments will always have less risk in a down market than simply being in the stock market alone.

- Unlike aging, with this investment the passage of time is your best friend, not your enemy!

- You get your twelve-percent or greater return *paid up front immediately* the day after you make your investment trade…no waiting as with other investments. And you can take that money and use it right away for your personal expenses or use it to reinvest and make even more money!

"Have you heard of another investment that can make all of those claims…an investment *less risky than the stock market alone* where *time is on your side* and where you get *your investment return paid out to you before you actually earn it*?" Max asked.

Both Ernie's and Karie's jaws dropped visibly. Finally Ernie said, "Max, you are going to have to do a lot of explaining to get me to understand how all that can be accomplished!"

"Well, that sounds like an invitation to begin. Are you both ready?"

Ernie and Karie looked at each other and nodded their heads eagerly, settling into their chairs. Ernie did have one reservation, however, and he expressed it. "Max," he said with a bit of a pained look on his face, "I've always been taught that if something seems too good to be true, there's probably a downside. Is there a downside to this?"

Max smiled and responded. "Ernie, I guess you could say there is, and we'll talk about it at the right point in our discussion. But even if the downside occurs on a given investment using this program, you will still make more, likely a lot more, than an annualized return of twelve-percent on your investment."

Ernie again could hardly believe what he was hearing, but eagerly said, "OK, Max, you've hit the ball out of the stadium. Now I'm really ready!"

Max sat back into his chair and began. "I know what I have told you about this program up to now sounds very exciting…and it is. But describing the details of how it works may actually seem somewhat boring. In thinking through how to present the program to you, I thought about what Elizabeth Taylor's *last* husband must have felt on their wedding night. He knew what he wanted to do…he just didn't know how to make it interesting! That's my challenge too, because I certainly want to keep you interested so you can implement the program…with apologies for the analogy!" Max said, displaying a slightly red face.

Karie let out a muted, half-hearted chuckle. "Max, I've never yet known a banker who could tell a joke. We promise we will stay interested. If your program will do most of what you have said, we'll get through it, even if it is boring. Frankly, what it sounds like to me is not boring, but mysterious!"

"That will be my challenge," Max announced, "…to demystify it for you."

PRACTICAL APPLICATIONS FOR MAKING MONEY

The PC CD/ROM included on the back cover of this book contains a number of Microsoft® Excel files that may help determine how you can reach your financial goals. Based upon your objectives, they will help guide you in assessing the amounts you need to regularly save, what rates of return you need in order to achieve your goals and other valuable information. Below is a listing of file names, what they will accomplish for you and how to use them. Place the CD/ROM in your computer and bring up each Excel file individually. Customize the input for each file to fit your individual situation to help in your planning. Transfer these files to your hard drive, as you may wish to use them on occasion by inputting different information.

File Name: Future_Value_LessTax
Purpose: Allows you to compute the future value of a lump-sum investment with annual savings additions that grow each year with your income. Income taxes are also calculated into the results. Note that when the input is completed, the program provides a detailed schedule of information at the bottom by year for forty years.
How to use the file (fields of information to complete):

- Number of years savings will occur – enter the number of years until your retirement

- Annualized rate of return on investment – enter the return you think you can achieve
- Current investment value – enter the current balance of your investment assets
- Amount of annual savings addition – enter the amount you can add to your investment each year
- Percent of growth of future savings additions – if you expect your salary or other income will be increasing annually, you can enter a percentage amount by which your annual investment addition will grow each year
- Marginal (highest) tax rate – enter the tax bracket percentage into which any new income would be taxed (obtain from government tax tables). You can combine the percentages for Federal and state.

File Name: Future_Value_LumpSum
Purpose: Allows you to compute the future value of a lump-sum investment at different interest rates and for a series of years. Note that a schedule of asset values is provided by year for forty years.
How to use the file (fields of information to complete):
- Amount of lump sum investment – enter the current balance of your investment assets or another lump sum amount you wish to review
- Compounding periods per year – leave at 1 unless you have assets that compound quarterly (enter 4), monthly (enter 12) or some other compounding period
- Interest rates – replace the current rates (from 4% to 20%) with any number you wish

File Name: Future_Value_Savings

Purpose: Allows you to compute the future value of regular savings additions.

How to use the file (fields of information to complete):

- Amount of regular savings additions – enter the amount you expect to save at each savings period
- Annualized rate of return on investment – enter the return you think you can achieve
- Number of years savings will occur – enter the number of years to your retirement
- Number of savings additions per year – enter the number of times you will make savings additions each year

File Name: Inflation_Return

Purpose: Allows you to compute an after-inflation rate of return.

How to use the file (fields of information to complete):

- Annualized rate of return on investment – enter the return you think you can achieve
- Inflation rate (Consumer Price Index) – enter the current rate of inflation

File Name: Return_Rate

Purpose: Allows you to compute the rate of return required to achieve an investment goal.

How to use the file (fields of information to complete):

- Desired future investment value – enter the value of the investment you wish to achieve
- Current investment value – enter the current balance of your investment assets
- Number of years to achieve investment – enter the number of years to your goal (retirement, for example)

- Compounding periods per year – leave at 1 unless you have assets that compound quarterly (enter 4), monthly (enter 12) or some other compounding period

File Name: Savings_Required
Purpose: Allows you to compute the periodic savings amount required to achieve a future investment.
How to use the file (fields of information to complete):
- Desired future investment value – enter the value of the investment you wish to achieve
- Annualized rate of return on investment – enter the return you think you can achieve
- Number of years to achieve investment – enter the number of years to your goal (retirement, for example)
- Number of savings additions per year – enter the number of times you will make savings additions each year

File Name: Time_Required
Purpose: Allows you to compute the time required to grow a current investment to a goal.
How to use the file (fields of information to complete):
- Annualized rate of return on investment – enter the return you think you can achieve
- Current investment value – enter the current balance of your investment assets
- Desired future investment value – enter the value of the investment you wish to achieve
- Compounding periods per year – leave at 1 unless you have assets that compound quarterly (enter 4), monthly (enter 12) or some other compounding period

File Name: Years_Deposits

Purpose: Allows you to compute the number of years and the number of savings additions required to achieve an investment goal.

How to use the file (fields of information to complete):

- Amount of regular savings additions – enter the amount you expect to save at each savings period

- Desired future investment value – enter the value of the investment you wish to achieve

- Annualized rate of return on investment – enter the return you think you can achieve

- Number of savings additions per year – enter the number of times you will make savings additions each year

Always bear in mind

that your own resolution

to succeed

is more important

than any other one thing.

Abraham Lincoln

5

THE GURU REVEALS HIS "SECRET"

> When I was a boy of fourteen, my father was so ignorant I could hardly stand to have the old man around. But when I got to be twenty-one, I was astonished at how much he had learned in seven years.
>
> Unknown

"Through this program," Max stated with emphasis, "I will give you the theoretical and practical tools necessary to develop an investment discipline that will help you achieve your goal of twelve-percent or greater returns on your investments through '**covered call option writing**' on common stocks."

Max paused a bit to let it sink in. "Do the words '**call**' or '**option**' mean anything to either of you?" he asked.

Karie turned to Ernie with a puzzled look on her face. Something flashed into Ernie's mind and he said, "Well, I've heard some people say when they hear the word 'option' they think of high risk... where a person might lose their entire investment," Ernie responded.

"Actually, that can be very true," Max agreed, "...but I promise you here and now...that has NOTHING to do with the investment program we will be talking about for you. Quite the opposite. In fact, the covered call option writing program we will be using can take big losses by others and turn them into your profits! The investment *for them may be high risk*, but *your investment is very conservative* as you will soon see."

"OK, I'm in so far," Karie acknowledged. "But what do you mean by '**covered**'?"

"That simply means that you own the stock that stands behind the options…that you have the stock to deliver if it is sold. I know that doesn't mean much to you now, but it will a little later, OK?"

"As long as you explain it later, Max. I have the feeling it would only confuse me more if we went into it further now," Karie said, a bit puzzled. "So, is there also such a thing as '**uncovered**'?"

"Yes, there is, Karie," Max countered, with a serious look on his face. "I can assure you that you won't have anything to do with that, though. It's an extremely high-risk strategy. It means you are writing calls on stock that you don't own. Suffice it to say that there is the potential for unlimited losses. How does that sound?"

"Let's move on quickly, Max!" Karie responded with wide eyes.

"And how about '**writing**'?" Ernie asked further.

"As you'll see shortly, Ernie, the term 'writing' when used in conjunction with covered calls simply means selling…you are selling calls on stock you own. But let's slow down a minute and regroup."

THE KEY DISCUSSION TOPICS

Max continued. "Our discussions about this program will revolve around these subjects: what covered call options are and how they work; how and where they are traded; thoughts on selection decisions for stocks on which to write options; how to decide which covered calls to write; using short-term technical indicators to assess market direction; how to use an Excel spreadsheet template I created to assist you in those decisions; how to select and use a broker to execute your transactions; how to evaluate your success in meeting your investment program goals; some information on tax matters; and a discussion of some fundamental economic considerations. But I'm getting ahead of myself. If we are going to get into all of these subjects, there has to be a discussion first of some additional new terms and how they are defined. This is where it may get a bit boring, but it's absolutely essential."

"Max, if it helps us get to twelve-percent how boring can it be?" Ernie joked. Karie smiled and obviously agreed.

Max continued. "The program involves the use of an investment referred to as an **'option contract,'** which defines the rights and obligations of the parties involved. There are only three actions investors need to take with this program to achieve their investment objectives using covered call option contracts:

- Select appropriate common stocks on which call options can be written.
- Select the specific covered call option contracts to be written.
- Initiate the trades.

"This cycle is then repeated over and over.

"Our discussion will primarily revolve around the details behind the second and third actions, although we will also deal with some philosophical approaches to appropriate common stock selection and economic factors that affect them. This program requires that you already have some knowledge of the stock markets and either know what stocks you want to own or have the ability to do some research and make decisions, preferably making use of an investment advisory service, as we were discussing earlier. I think we agreed that this is not an issue with you folks, right?" Max asked.

(Reader/Investor: If you feel you are in need of an education or a refresher on stocks and the markets, please refer to the appropriate suggested readings and Internet Web sites listed in the Appendix.)

"That's right," Ernie responded. "In fact, we took your suggestions and signed up for both the Zacks Advisor and Value Line trial services since we met last. I just have one problem. Since we did that, I can't get on my computer anymore because Karie is always busy looking up information about stocks on their Internet Web sites!" Ernie laughed.

"That's true!" retorted Karie. "It's your fault, Max. You sure picked a couple of very interesting investment services. They are really informative and I've got some good new ideas to discuss with Ernie already," Karie reported.

"Great. That's what they are for. But you'd better let Ernie on now and then. I don't want to be responsible for any marital conflict!" Max chuckled.

"I said earlier that this program, covered call option writing, is not a secret at all. It's been done for decades. Nobody talks much about it though, and most people aren't involved in it. But it is widely accepted by many knowledgeable individual and 'institutional investors.' In fact, any reputable full-service or discount brokerage company can verify the validity and usefulness of writing covered calls on stocks. They provide brokerage services not only for stocks, but also for options as part of what they do for their customers."

"Institutional investors?" Karie repeated with a confused look. "What's that?"

Max was ready. "Well, Karie, it's anybody who bought technology stocks at the top of the market, rode them all the way down, and is now in an insane asylum!" Max chuckled out loud. "No, actually, the term refers to mutual funds, bank trust departments, insurance companies, brokerage firms, pension funds...that sort of very large investor."

Karie was starting to get used to the idea that Max was determined to inject humor to alleviate his concerns about the subject matter being too boring for them. She let him know that was fine and laughed out loud with Ernie.

"You might be interested in knowing that many institutional investors use covered call option writing as an important part of their investing strategy."

Ernie had a puzzled look on his face. "If you can trade both stocks and covered call options through a broker, then why don't more people just let their stockbrokers advise them about writing covered calls on their stocks?"

"The reason is very simple, Ernie. Few brokerage firms I have ever known of give their individual customers all of the information they need to carry out the objectives we will discuss. We'll talk more about brokerage accounts later. For now, suffice it to say that you can use a 'live' retail broker to execute your investment transactions, or, much better in my opinion, conduct your investment business over the Internet or by touch-tone phone through a discount broker. You will need a brokerage firm to handle the transactions so you can carry out the program. But I am not aware of many full-service brokerage firms that give detailed information to their clients on how to go about it and will also walk you through the entire process of covered call writing as we will do in our discussions. Also, full-service brokerages usually charge commissions many times as great as discount brokers for both stock and option trades.

The problem with using a stockbroker, actually called a 'registered representative,' of a full-service brokerage firm is that they are not usually knowledgeable about such investment opportunities. They are essentially sales people. Some are geared to a long-term 'buy-and-hold' approach for common stocks only. And, of course, some try to do a lot of trading for their customers. They are, after all, paid through trade commissions."

"I can relate to that," Karie responded. "Before Ernie and I were married I had a really strange stockbroker. He seemed to be more interested in selling me something and trading it than in making money for me."

"Funny you should mention that. It reminds me of a story!" Max said excitedly. "There was this stockbroker who died by the name of Strange. His friend asked the tombstone maker to inscribe on his tombstone, 'Here lies Strange, an honest man, and a stockbroker.' The inscriber insisted that such an inscription would be confusing, because passers-by would tend to think that three men were buried under the same stone. However, he suggested an alternative. He said he would inscribe, 'Here lies a man who was both honest and a stockbroker.' That way, whenever anyone walked by the tombstone and read it, they would be certain to remark, 'That's Strange!'"

"Oh, Max!" Karie retorted, while rolling her eyes. "More banker jokes?"

"That was a stockbroker joke. Sorry, I don't get a chance to use these very often! So you don't think I can make it as a standup comedian?" Max asked.

"I'd keep your day job if I were you, Max!" Ernie retorted with a laugh.

"I don't mean to disparage stockbrokers," Max continued after composing himself. "For the right person they can perform very valuable services. It's just that most of them don't know much about the program we will be talking about, and for a knowledgeable investor it can readily be self-initiated with a great deal of money saved."

"We'll I'm glad of that. And we already use a discount broker for our investments," Karie was quick to point out.

"So much the better. That will make it very easy. But again, we are getting ahead of ourselves. I'm anxious to get back to the boring part!" Max quipped.

THE "SECRET" IN A NUTSHELL

"Here's a highly abridged version of what this is all about," Max began. "You will not be *buying* call options, which is a potentially high-risk strategy, but rather you will be *selling* call options on common stocks you already own or will acquire, also known as *writing*. This is a very conservative, yet potentially lucrative option investing strategy. When you sell an option on stock that you own you are selling a window of time in which the buyer has the right to buy your stock at a set price. The buyer is hoping that your stock is going to go up significantly during this window of time that the option is active...in other words, before the option expires. When you sell an option on your stock, you are performing a transaction known as 'writing a covered call,' or, more simply 'writing calls,' or just 'call writing.' By writing covered calls, you can reduce the downside risk on your investment, you can predict with greater accuracy how much money you will make, and you can help stabilize your profits. Selling the right to buy your stock to other people gives you the ability to make consistent and significant returns on your investments, and the buyer immediately pays you money to do this, as we shall see."

"You will be providing more explanation, right?" Ernie asked with a blank look on his face.

"Of course. I realize that's a mouthful, but it's the essence of it. You may not understand much about it now, but by the time we get through some definitions, examples and calculations, you will become much more comfortable with how it works. It will become second nature to you and you'll be ready to start making money with the program.

"Ernie and Karie, I'm going to get through some other important terms and their definitions by posing them as questions to you and then answering the questions. These terms are important because we will be using some of them a lot going forward. Being sure you understand them precisely will allow us to converse more easily as you advance in your ability to use this covered call option writing program. I'm going to give you a list of all of these terms and their definitions too."

(Reader/Investor: An alphabetical listing of the terms appearing in bold type and their definitions is located in the Glossary.)

"As we go through the terms, please don't hesitate to interrupt me and ask questions of your own at any time," Max stated.

"Sure, Max," said Ernie, "but you presume that with all you've thrown at me my mind is working well enough to ask an intelligent question. Be patient with me, Max. My mind works like lightening. One brilliant flash and it's gone!"

Max broke out into laughter. "I've got to remember that one, Ernie. Well, you will become increasingly intelligent on this subject as we go on...both of you. These are questions you are sure to ask anyway, so we might as well get them out of the way. Just stop me if there is anything about what I'm saying that you don't understand."

"You can be sure of that!" Karie responded.

"Very good," said Max. "Here's the first question:

JUST WHAT IS AN OPTION?

"The *buyer* of an option has the right, but not the obligation, to buy or sell a stock for a specified price on or before a specific date. A 'call' is the right to *buy* the stock...like calling it away from you...while a 'put' is the right of a stock owner to *sell* the stock...like putting it into your hands. The investor who purchases an option, whether it is a call or a put, is the option buyer. Conversely, the person who initiates a transaction by selling a call is the call option *seller* or *writer*, as I've said before. The buyer of the option is *not* obligated to buy the stock, but the seller *is* obligated to sell if the buyer decides to 'exercise' his right of purchase under the option. When the buyer of a call exercises the option, the seller's stock is said to be 'assigned,' meaning it will be sold. In the case of our investment program, you will *always* be the seller of options. And we will only be dealing with calls, not puts. The subject of puts will not be brought up again.

WHERE DO I TRADE COVERED CALL OPTIONS?

"Option contracts are considered to be securities. As such, they are bought and sold through a brokerage firm. As we said, either a full-service brokerage or a discount brokerage can be used, although option trades through a discount broker are usually much less expensive. Option contracts trade on U.S. securities exchanges, such as the Chicago Board Options Exchange (CBOE), the American Stock Exchange (ASE), the Philadelphia Stock Exchange (PHLX) and the Pacific Stock Exchange (PSE) . The contracts traded on all of the exchanges are issued, guaranteed and cleared, that is to say settled or finalized, by the **'Options Clearing Corporation (OCC).'** The OCC is a registered clearing corporation with the **'Securities & Exchange Commission (SEC).'** It's not necessary to understand any more than that, except that this provides you with needed protection to assure your transactions fit certain common standards and that they all are handled through an independent and unbiased third party.

WHAT ARE SOME OF THE WELL-KNOWN STOCKS OFFERING CALL OPTIONS?

"There are literally thousands of stocks on which covered call writing can be done. Here are just a very few of the more recognizable company names whose stocks you can use to write call options." Max handed Ernie and Karie a list, which read as follows:

American Express (AXP)	Anheuser Busch (BUD)	AOL Time/Warner (AOL)
Atlantic Richfield (ARC)	AT&T (T)	Bank of America (BAC)
Best Buy (BBY)	Chevron/Texaco (CVX)	Cisco Systems (CSCO)
Citigroup (C)	Coca Cola (KO)	Colgate-Palmolive (CL)
Dell Computer (DELL)	Disney (DIS)	Eastman Kodak (EK)
FedEx (FDX)	Ford Motor (F)	The Gap (GPS)
General Electric (GE)	General Motors (GM)	Hewlett Packard (HWP)
Home Depot (HD)	IBM (IBM)	Intel (INTC)
Johnson & Johnson (JNJ)	Kimberly-Clark (KMB)	McDonald's (MCD)
Merck (MRK)	Merrill Lynch (MER)	Microsoft (MSFT)
3M (MMM)	Monsanto (MTC)	Morgan/Chase(JPM)
Motorola (MOT)	Nokia (NOK)	Pfizer (PFE)
Safeway (SWY)	Schering-Plough (SGP)	Texaco (TX)
Wal-Mart (WMT)	Wells Fargo (WFC)	Yahoo (YHOO)

"Obviously these are names I recognize. So I could write call options on any of these?" Ernie inquired.

"That's right," Max responded, "And a whole lot more than you would ever believe!"

HOW DO I MAKE MONEY
WRITING COVERED CALLS?

"You can make money three ways. First, you are always paid cash, called a '**premium**,' for giving someone the right to buy your shares from you at a specific price, which is called the '**strike price**,' on or before the '**expiration date**' when the option expires. You get to keep the premium money whether or not the shares are actually bought from you later. There are typically a variety of strike prices available, some of which will usually be below the current market price of the stock and some of which will be above it. There are also a variety of option expiration dates available that extend out as short as the current and the next month to about three years for options on some stocks. These very long-term options, whose expirations range from one to about three years, are referred to as **'LEAPS,'** which stands for 'Long-Term Equity Anticipation Securities.' They are traded through your broker the same as other options.

"Second, I almost always suggest that the strike price on the options you write be *higher* than the current market value of the stock on which you are writing options. This is referred to as being **'out-of-the-money.'** For example, if the current price of the stock on which you are writing options is $28 and you write an option with a $30 strike price, the option is said to be out-of-the-money by $2. This means, in addition to the premium income, you can also potentially receive additional **'capital appreciation.'** That's the difference between the price of a stock when a call option is written and the strike price of the call option. Your stock would likely be sold, that is to say 'called away from you,' or 'assigned,' if the price of the stock is above $30 per share on the option expiration date. You would get to keep your option premium, plus your stock would be called away at $30 per share, which is $2 per share greater than it was when you wrote the call option.

"Third, if your stocks pay dividends, you have that source of income as well."

"So, if you are writing options on stocks you own, you still get to keep the dividends?" Ernie asked.

"Absolutely," Max responded. "You are the owner of the stock during the option period, so any dividends that are declared with an ex-dividend date taking place when you own the stock means the dividends belong to you...and that obviously enhances your yield as you combine it with the option writing income and any capital appreciation to calculate your total yield."

"That makes sense," Ernie noted.

"If you were to write an option with a strike price *lower* than the current price of the stock, the option is said to be **'in-the-money.'** For example, if the current price of the stock is $32 and you write an option with a $30 strike price, the option is said to be in-the-money by $2. As we will see later, you would receive a higher premium by writing an in-the-money option when compared to an out-of-the-money option, but you could actually incur a loss on your stock compared with its price on the date you wrote the option if you write the in-the-money option. If the price in this example remained the same, you would receive only $30 per share for stock that was worth $32 at the time you wrote the option, or a loss of $2 per share from the market price at the time the option was written. You would rarely, if ever, want to do this.

"Finally, when the market price of a stock is exactly the same as the strike price of a given option, or very close, the option is said to be **'at-the-money.'** An example of this would be if you were interested in a call option with a strike price of $25 and the **'underlying stock,'** that is to say the stock you own on which you would be writing the call options, was selling at exactly $25 per share.

"Now I know this must be sounding very confusing. Hold on tight a little longer and we will simplify all this with more detailed examples.

WHAT ARE STRIKE PRICES
AND HOW ARE THEY DETERMINED?

"A strike price is the actual price at which the buyer of the option has the right to purchase the stock covered by the option. Typically each stock that trades options offers at least several different strike prices for each expiration date. Strike prices are established when the underlying stock either advances or declines to a certain price level and trades consistently at or above that level. If, for example, JJJ stock was trading at $49, hit a price of $50 and traded consistently at this level, a new and higher strike price may be added by the exchange where the option is traded. Volatile stocks that trade in a broader range of prices would have more strike prices available for selection, some of which would be above the current market price for the stock and some of which would be below. Strike prices are typically established in $5 increments, although $2 ½ increments are often used, particularly when the stock price is lower.

"AOL/Time Warner stock, for example, has traded in a very wide range. Different expiration dates sometimes have different strike prices that go along with them. As of now the following strike prices are available for at least some of the expirations for AOL/Time Warner: $7 ½, $10, $12 ½, $15, $17 ½, $20, $22 ½, $25, $27 ½ , $30, $32 ½, $35, $37 ½, $40, $42 ½, $45, $47 ½ , $50, $55, $60, $65, $70, $75, $80, $85, $90, $95, $100, $105, $110, $115, $120, $125, $130, $135, $140, $145 and $150. This gives you some idea of the wide range in which AOL has traded for so many strike prices to have been created."

"I'm glad I missed out on buying that stock at the time the $150 strike price was being created!" Ernie sighed with obvious relief.

WHEN DO I GET THE PREMIUM INCOME MONEY?

"Once you've written a call," Max continued, "the cash premium is deposited into your brokerage account THE NEXT BUSINESS DAY, even though you have not earned it yet. That's one of the many attractive benefits of this program that I mentioned to you earlier. No waiting! The premium is paid to you in cash...and, it is yours to use or invest *now* to earn even more money for yourself."

"That's sure a big difference from waiting around for your interest to be paid on a bank CD or bond, isn't it?" Karie added.

"CDs and bonds have their proper place, of course. But, you are right," the Guru acknowledged.

WHAT IS THE EXPIRATION DATE?

"The expiration date is the last day on which an option may be exercised by the option buyer. This date is officially the Saturday immediately following the third Friday of the expiration month. If Friday is a holiday, the last trading day will be the preceding Thursday.

WHAT IF THE STOCK I WRITE A CALL ON DROPS SIGNIFICANTLY IN PRICE?

"Obviously a decline in a stock's price can happen to anyone. If it couldn't, everyone in the world would invest everything they have in the stock market. If the drop is due to very bad company news, it could be best to buy back the call at a profit and sell the stock immediately before further price decreases occur. When you write call options on a stock and the stock price goes down, the price of the option goes down too, which is good news for the call writer. You could then buy the options back at a lower price than you sold them for and realize a profit on the difference. Or you can wait until expiration when the calls would be worthless. Then you've realized the entire premium income as gain. That's how the downside protection comes into play.

"Just like stocks, call options are traded continuously on the exchanges. This is because option contracts, like stocks, are 'fungible' assets. That means you can buy and sell the same option contract at any time prior to expiration, because the contracts are identical and are interchangeable with other investors on the exchanges where they are traded.

"The bid and ask prices of the option change too, even from minute to minute, as the price of the underlying stock changes and as the time to expiration becomes shorter so there is less time remaining. We will talk more about strategies for a declining stock price later. Just keep in mind that if a stock declines you will *always* be better off if you have written call options on it than if you just owned the stock by itself, because the premium you receive gives you some 'downside protection.'

WHAT IF THE STOCK I WRITE A CALL ON SHOOTS WAY UP IN PRICE?

"I admitted earlier that there is a downside. I don't consider a declining stock price a downside to writing covered calls, because you presumably already own stocks and the premium you receive gives you some protection against a declining stock price. In other words, you are better off than if you just owned the stock. The downside for the option writer occurs when the stock price shoots up way above your strike price plus the option premium received and is in that position on the expiration date. In such a case, the option writer would have been better off just owning the stock and not writing the options.

"But, while the option writer may have lost in the sense that the call writing transaction didn't capture the entire rise in the stock, by receiving the premium income plus the gain up to the strike price, the investor has obtained the maximum objective sought when the calls were initially written. Now I would say that's a downside with an upside!

"If your stock goes way up, there are some choices, which we will be covering in more detail. You can wait to see if your stock gets called away from you at expiration. Another choice is to buy back the call at what could be a higher price than you initially sold it for. By doing this you release your obligation to sell the stock, but I hardly ever recommend that strategy, as we will discuss later.

WHAT IF MY SHARES DON'T GET CALLED AWAY AT EXPIRATION?

"It varies, but experts suggest that about eighty-percent of the time options written out-of-the-money expire without being exercised. If the expiration date comes and goes and your stock was not called away, this means you still own the stock and you have earned the premium. You can then sell the stock at its current market value, just continue to hold the stock, or write another call and collect another premium.

UNDER WHAT CIRCUMSTANCES WILL MY STOCK LIKELY BE CALLED AWAY?

"You can anticipate having your stock called away, referred to as being 'assigned,' when your option becomes 'in-the-money.' This almost always occurs at expiration if the market price of the stock is greater than the strike price, although it could possibly happen at any time during the term of the option contract if the buyer of the option wanted to exercise the right earlier.

IF THE CALLS I WRITE EXPIRE WITHOUT BEING EXERCISED AND I GET TO KEEP ALL OF THE PREMIUM INCOME, DO I HAVE TO PAY A COMMISSION AT EXPIRATION?

"No. As a writer of call options, the only time you pay an option commission is when you initiate the transaction or close out your position by buying it back. I almost never recommend closing it out. If the option expires worthless, as a call writer you keep the entire option premium and pay no additional commission at expiration."

Karie appeared to be a bit worried. "Max," she said, "I understand only a little bit of what you've said so far. I'm not sure I can go on and get this if I can't even follow it up to now."

Max shot her a reassuring smile. "Karie, we aren't going any further with this until you understand all that I've said so far. And the best way to help you understand is with some examples that support these terms and definitions. This is a very good time to get into this. Tell, me, what stock represents your single largest holding other than our company stock?"

"That would be KKK Industries," Ernie responded.

PRACTICAL APPLICATIONS FOR MAKING MONEY

One of the most popular Web sites on the Internet is Yahoo!. Yahoo! is more than just a search engine. It's a "portal." As such, it provides an entry point within itself to a huge menu of additional sites and information. Go to www.yahoo.com and click on "Finance/Quotes." You will see a box titled "Enter one or more symbols." Inside that box, type the stock ticker symbols for stocks you own or wish to research, separated by commas but no spaces. Then click on "Get." If you don't know the symbol for the stock you want, you can click on "Symbol Lookup" and you will be taken to a page to find the symbol.

As you look at the page, you will see the latest trade and volume information for these stocks. In addition, on the right are a number of links on which you can click that will provide a great deal more information. By clicking on "Chart" you will see a chart of the stock's price movements along with other data. Clicking on "News" will give you many additional links, sorted by date, for both printed and audio news of all kinds on the company. Clicking on "Profile" provides a summary of business and financial information. You can buy a variety of available brokerage reports on the company by clicking on "Reports." Clicking on "Research" will provide a summary of broker recommendations on the company as well as past earnings,

earnings estimates and price targets for the stock. Clicking on "Insider" gives insider and restricted shareholder trading information. "Options" will provide a list of many of the call and put options that are traded on the stock and their latest prices, bid, ask, volume, and "open interest," which is the total number of contracts currently outstanding for that particular option contract. Finally, clicking on "Msgs" will take you to the message board for that stock where everyone in the world can freely express their opinion about the company, or just about anything else…no holds barred!

This is but one of an uncountable number of sites and portals from which you can seek investment information. Just remember…caveat emptor!

And here are the stock quotes for the day.....

Helium was up.

Feathers were down.

Paper was stationary.

Fluorescent tubing was dimmed in light trading.

Knives were up sharply.

Cows steered into a bull market.

Pencils lost a few points.

Hiking equipment was trailing.

Elevators rose, while escalators continued their slow decline.

Weights were up in heavy trading.

Light switches were off.

Mining equipment hit rock bottom.

Diapers remain unchanged.

Shipping lines stayed at an even keel.

The market for raisins dried up.

Coca Cola fizzled.

Caterpillar stock inched up a bit.

Sun peaked at midday.

Balloon prices were inflated.

And, Scott Tissue touched a new bottom.

6

EXAMPLES AND MORE EXAMPLES

> For those who like this sort
> of thing, this is the sort of
> thing they like.
>
> Abraham Lincoln

"To really understand what *you* will be doing through covered call option writing we need to start by looking first at a typical call transaction from the *buyer's* perspective. That side of the transaction has absolutely nothing directly to do with what you will be doing, but understanding the 'buy' side of the transaction will greatly help you understand the 'sell' side, which is *your* side. For purposes of simplicity, I'm not going to include commissions in any of the following examples. I have not found any way yet to completely avoid paying commissions on stock and option trades, so later we will discuss how you can keep commissions down to a reasonable minimum. But for now, just remember that there will be some commissions involved that will affect these numbers a bit.

THE CALL BUYER'S (SPECULATOR'S)
SIDE OF THE TRANSACTION

"Let's say KKK Industries ('ticker symbol' 'KKK') common stock is selling for $50 per share at the end of January. 'John,' as we will call the buyer, thinks KKK may be poised to rise, so he buys ten KKK call contracts with a June expiration and with a strike price of $55 per share. For this he pays a premium of, let's say, $3 per contract. Each call contract covers 100 shares of the underlying stock, unless later adjusted for a stock split or stock dividend. So during the term of this option John controls 1,000 shares of KKK. The price he pays for this, the option premium, is $3,000 ($3 premium per contract x 10 contracts x 100 shares per contract)."

"Excuse me, Max," Karie interjected, "but how was it determined that the option premium would be $3?"

"That's a great question, Karie. It is based on mathematical formulations and largely revolves around the price volatility of the underlying stock, how far the strike price of the option is from the current price of KKK stock, and how much time exists between now and the time the option will expire," Max responded. "Let me explain how each of those factors operate."

"The more volatile a given stock's recent price history in the marketplace, the higher the premium a call will command. For example, all other things being equal, a call on many of the high-flying tech stocks, which experience substantial price swings, would typically have a premium greater than KKK Industry's options. In turn, KKK Industry's options would logically have a premium that would be higher than a less volatile stock...say, for example, most public utility stocks.

"Second, the price of the stock relative to the strike price of the option is a major factor. If the price of KKK is $50 per share, it only needs to trade $5 per share higher to reach a $55 strike price, while it would need to trade $10 higher to reach a $60 strike price. Since the likelihood is obviously much greater of the stock price reaching $55 by the end of the same expiration period than $60, the price of the option for a $55 strike will be significantly higher than the $60 strike. In other words, for out-of-the-money calls, the closer the strike price is to the current market price of the stock, the greater the call option premium will be.

"Third, if it is now March and you are writing an option, you will want more premium for a call that will expire in September than one that will expire in June, right? If you are giving the call buyer the option to buy your stock at a specific price until September, the buyer has a lot more time for the price to go up than if the option expires in June. For that reason, the buyer will have to pay quite a bit more for the September expiration than for the June expiration. Am I making sense to both of you?"

Both Ernie and Karie nodded affirmatively, but somewhat cautiously.

"The mathematical formulas are the framework behind the pricing of options for both buyer and seller. Ultimately, actual trading prices are established by what a willing buyer and willing seller agree upon.

"Another factor that can affect the level of option premiums is the economic environment. For example, let's say there is a rough market where prices have declined, recovered a bit, declined, and so on. There isn't much 'visibility' going forward regarding when the economy will improve and stock prices will recover. That scenario is reflected not only in stock prices, but also in option premiums. Option premiums for the same stocks, strike prices and expirations, when compared during different economic times, have sometimes trended lower in times of market uncertainty. In other words, the premiums you receive from writing options in that economic climate may not be quite as large as they were when the economy was more certain and the markets were performing better. The good news is that an investor can still find very acceptable option premiums to reach target investment objectives, and it is possible that when the economy improves and markets recover option premiums will improve as well, providing even better returns from option writing."

Max continued. "So, getting back to the KKK example, how does this work for John? The buyer of a call is a speculator. In this case John is speculating that the price of KKK stock will rise fairly quickly so he can take his profit. The call he has purchased will go up and down with the price of KKK stock."

It was Ernie who interrupted this time. "I'm not sure I understand that. Once the buyer buys a call and the seller sells a call, the price of the option goes up and down before the expiration date?"

"That's exactly right, Ernie. These option contracts, just like the underlying stock, both continue to be traded on the open market. In the short run, if the price of KKK stock would rise, then the price of the call contract should rise as well. And the price of the option would rise at a higher percentage rate than the stock itself, because the purchase of an option provides 'leverage'...100 shares for each contract. In this case, for a price of $3,000 John has control, for a limited period of time, of 1,000 shares of KKK stock worth $50,000. If KKK would rise to $55 the next day after the trade, the owner of the stock would have a gain for that day of 10%. The call option, however, might in turn rise to $4.50 or a gain of 50% above the option purchase price. The buyer, if he wished to, could then sell his option contracts on the open market and pocket his gain on the transaction. As we will see, this really has no effect on you and your option strategy. You will almost always just sit on your covered call options and wait for the expiration date to pass."

Ernie seemed puzzled. "But if John wants to sell his calls, wouldn't we have to be involved?"

"No, Ernie. Specific buyers and sellers of calls aren't matched together unless calls are assigned at expiration. Either party can get out of their call position through their broker, just like a stock trade. That's what makes options fungible.

"This demonstrates the reason why a speculator might choose to buy an option rather than buy the underlying stock. Had John purchased 1,000 shares of KKK at $50 and sold it at $55 his investment would have been $50,000 and his profit $5,000 for a return of 10%. By buying the option contracts instead, he realized a 50% profit on his investment but tied up only $3,000 of his capital in the process. This sounds terrific, but what's the downside? If KKK stock had declined from $50 to $45 the value of his options would also decline, perhaps going from $3 to $1.50. This would represent a loss of $1,500 or 50% of his investment. Had he bought the stock and it declined to $45, the percentage loss would only be 10%.

"By comparing ownership of stock with ownership of options one can begin to see the highly speculative nature of *buying* calls. Using options, a person can control a very large number of shares with very little money when compared with ownership of the underlying stock itself. This means the potential for big gains and big losses. There's another major difference between buying an option versus buying the stock. Options expire, but stocks do not. If an option buyer continues to hold the option, and if the price of the stock doesn't exceed the option 'strike price' at expiration, the options will always be completely worthless. So, if an investor is a buyer of call options, he not only has to be right about the stock going up, he has to be right about *when* it goes up!

"This is a good time to introduce two more terms into the discussion… **'intrinsic value'** and **'time value'** of options. We discussed the terms 'in-the-money,' 'out-of-the-money' and 'at-the-money' previously, which have to do with the relationship between the option strike price and the current market value of the stock on which options are being written. The 'intrinsic value' portion of an option's price is the dollar amount by which the strike price is less than the market price of the stock. For example, if a stock is trading at $47 ½ per share and the strike price of an option is $45, then the intrinsic value of the option is $2 ½. If the stock price and the strike price are the same, then the intrinsic value is $0. It is also $0 if the strike price is any amount greater than the market price. Obviously this can change at any given moment as the price of a stock moves up or down in trading. The strike price of a specific option is fixed until its expiration, but the market prices of the stock and the option normally change constantly as trading takes place. So a given option premium can have intrinsic value at times when the market price of the stock goes above the strike price and have no intrinsic value at times as well. As I have previously suggested, you will generally write options where the strike price is greater than the market price of the stock at the time of the trade, so there will be no intrinsic value when the option contracts are written.

"The 'time value' of an option premium is the market price of the option less the amount of intrinsic value. In other words, it is the value of the time remaining until the option expires. The longer the time between the current date and the expiration date the greater the time value of the option. This can be best understood through examples.

"Assume the following facts. You previously wrote a call option on AAA stock. The strike price is $55, the current market value of the stock is now $57 and the current price of the option is $4 ¼ . Since the market value now is higher than the strike price, the intrinsic value is determined by subtracting the strike price from the market price, which gives an intrinsic value of $2 for the premium. The time value is then determined by taking the current option price of $4 ¼ and subtracting the intrinsic value. The time value is therefore $4 ¼ minus $2 or $2 ¼. Another way to say this is that the *intrinsic value is the amount by which the stock is in-the-money*. The *time value is the rest of the price of the option.*

"Let's look at a second example. You have written a call option on JJJ stock. The strike price is $80, the current market value of the stock is $76 and the current price of the option is $3. The option is out-of-the-money, so there is no intrinsic value. Thus, the entire market price of the option premium of $3 is regarded as time value. Obviously this changes as the price of the stock and the option go up and down.

"Do either of you have questions about these definitions?" Max asked.

"Well, it seems a bit hazy right now, but I'm sure it will make sense later when we start using them," Karie responded optimistically, but in a bit of a daze.

"That's true. It will all come together for you then, I promise." Max continued. "So, back to KKK again. John stands to realize a substantial percentage profit or loss on his call option investment if there are short-term swings up or down in the market value of KKK stock. Let's examine what will happen if John continues to hold his option until the expiration date in June. You will recall that the strike price of the option contract John bought was $55. This means that on the expiration date if the price of KKK stock is less than $55 the options expire with no value. John has lost his entire investment. Why? John's option contracts give him the right, but not the obligation, to buy 1,000 shares of KKK for $55 per share at any time through the June expiration date. Options always expire on the Saturday following the third Friday of the expiration month. Generally options are not exercised until the expiration date and then, of course, only if they are in-the-money. The reason for that is simple. Option buyers are often speculators who really don't want to own the stock on a long-term basis or at all. Therefore, if the buyer of the option wants to close out his option position before the expiration, the buyer will almost always sell the contracts on the open market rather than exercise the options and then have to wait to sell the stock after it is delivered to his broker.

"But, in this case we are assuming John has not sold his option contracts and the June expiration date has just passed. We have said that if the price of KKK stock is below $55 he has lost his entire investment. What happens if after the expiration date the stock is above $55 per share? As we just said, John would have typically sold his contracts before expiration, but if the expiration date passes and the underlying stock market price is greater than the strike price, John should exercise his options and buy the stock because the options have intrinsic value. Let's say the price of KKK stock is $57 at the close of the market on the expiration date. If John exercises his options he will pay $55,000 for his 1,000 shares of KKK. By exercising his options he will have $57,000 worth of KKK stock which he can sell for a $2,000 profit.

"But wait! Didn't John pay $3,000 for the options and won't he still have a net loss by exercising the options and selling the stock? Yes…but the gain on the sale of the stock will partially offset the loss of the premium he paid ($2,000 investment gain - $3,000 premium loss = $1,000 net loss).

"Again, if John had held his options until around the expiration date he would have most likely sold the contracts themselves rather than exercise the options and sell the stock. Why? It is a much simpler transaction. By the time he could take delivery of the stock and sell it, the market price could possibly go down. If the stock was trading at $57 towards the end of the day on the last day of trading before expiration, the $55 KKK call option would be trading at about $2 per contract (time is up, so there is only the $2 intrinsic value and no time value is left). He would receive about $2,000 when he sold his ten contracts ($2 x 10 x 100), for the same result (except for commissions).

"When you remember that about eighty-percent of all options contracts that are out-of-the-money when the transaction is initiated expire worthless, it becomes clear that buying options is highly speculative. It requires significant price movement occurring rather quickly in the underlying stock if the buyer is to make a profit, especially if there isn't much time remaining to expiration.

"It is also clear that in many cases much or all of the option buyer's investment can be lost, even if the price of the underlying stock rises somewhat before the expiration date.

"Let's use the example of John's KKK options again. We'll say the price of KKK stock goes from $50 to $54 ¾ at expiration and John still holds his options. Even though the price of KKK stock has increased by $4 ¾, or 9.5%, in just about five months, John has still lost his entire investment. He would not exercise his option to buy shares at $55 that can be bought on the open market for $54 ¾. He has lost the premium he paid for the options. What is John's breakeven point on the expiration date? If he paid $3 per share premium to buy each contract, and if the strike price is $55, then John's breakeven is $58 per share ($3 + $55 = $58). In other words, if John holds the options through the expiration date, unless the price of KKK stock is at least $58 per share, or 16% higher than when he bought the options, he lost money. Of course, he could have sold the contracts well before the expiration date and made or lost money, depending on what the price of KKK stock and his options were and also how much of his time had run out before expiration.

"Are you beginning to see why the opposite, mirror side of this transaction, fortunately the side in which you will be involved as a covered call writer, is the more attractive proposition?"

Ernie was quick to respond. "Well, at this point I certainly do understand why *buying* call options isn't for us." Karie rolled her eyes in full agreement. "But I am anxious to hear more about how the seller's side of this can work for us."

THE CALL WRITER'S (YOUR) SIDE
OF THE TRANSACTION

"Right," Max said. "Let's look at the same transaction from YOUR side now. You are the owner of 1,000 shares of KKK Industries. You would like to increase your income by writing some call options on the shares you own. While you like the company's long-term prospects, you doubt that the price of the stock will go any higher than $5 above its current market price of about $50 over the next few months. It is about the end of January and you start checking out the premiums for KKK options contracts with various different strike prices and expiration dates. One of them that looks attractive to you is the June $55 KKK call. It is trading at, again let's say, $3 per contract. For receiving a premium of $3 per share you decide you would be willing to let go of your 1,000 shares of KKK at $55 per share if the price should be greater than $55 on the expiration date. Remember that the option buyer could call your shares away from you at any time up to and including the expiration date, but this rarely ever happens before the expiration date, even if the market price of the stock goes above the strike price.

"Using your computer, you plug all the data into the Excel option spreadsheet I mentioned earlier and read the following:

DATE------>	29-Jan														
X	X	X			X	X	X		X	X					
											$	PREM.		TOTAL	MAX.	ANNUAL
CO.	#	SHARE	MARKET		OPTION			OPTION		PREM.	$ PER	CONT.	ANNUAL	CAP.	YIELD W/
SYM.	SHS.	PRICE	VALUE	DIV.	EXPIR.	STRIKE	DAYS	SYMBOL	PREM.	INC.	DAY	YIELD	YIELD	APP.	CAP. APP.
KKK	1,000	$50.00	$50,000	$0.64	15-Jun	$55.00	137	KKKFJ	$3.00	$3,000	$21.90	6.00%	17.27%	$5,000	43.91%

"We will get into the details of the spreadsheet later, but trust me for now. From this transaction you will collect $3,000 in option writing income ($3 premium per share x 10 contracts x 100 shares per contract, not including commissions). You see that, on an annualized basis, the premium income and dividends at the current market price of KKK will yield 17.27%. Not bad! That's quite a bit higher than your annual return objective of 12%, and it will be locked in until June 15 (the third Friday in June) based upon that premium and the market price of the stock on the day of the transaction. We'll talk about the significance of the annualized yield again later. We use it for comparison purposes, as everyone is used to thinking in annual terms. When you buy a six-month CD at the bank at a 5% rate of interest, for example, the rate quoted is on an annual basis. If they quoted you 2 ½% for the six months, that would be comparable to the contract yield of 6% in this example.

"You also have the potential to realize an additional $5,000 of capital appreciation if the stock goes up to or over $55 per share on the expiration date. You can see that the total return on an annualized basis, which is the premium income, plus dividends, plus additional capital appreciation if the stock is called away from you at expiration, is 43.91%.

"Now the downside. If KKK stock would go to, say, $60 before the expiration date, you would probably feel pretty bad that you had lost out on some additional capital appreciation. You would only receive $55 per share plus your option premium of $3, or a total of $58 per share, so you would have missed out on receiving $2 per share that your stock would have been worth had you done nothing but hold it. Yet you realized an annualized return substantially in excess of your annualized return objective. You also had $3 per share of downside protection if KKK's stock price had headed south. I'd take that kind of downside on every transaction I do, as it would assure much better returns than the objective. Some transactions will turn out like that. You just have to remember that you are no longer in the business of maximizing capital appreciation on any given stock. You are in the business of using covered call options to provide you a rate of return that will meet or exceed your objective. If you keep that in mind, you will not be disappointed, even if your stock is called away from you at times. An even more frequent occurrence would be that your stock is called away, but the strike price plus the premium you receive is greater than the market value of the stock at expiration. This means you are better off than if you had just held the stock.

"This points out that we can't just look at the call option premium income in isolation. We have to consider what happens to the stock price too in figuring our overall return. Obviously it can go down too. We'll address that shortly.

"Anyway, you decide to go ahead and place an order to 'sell-to-open' ten contracts of the KKK June $55 calls at $3. "

"What do you mean by 'sell-to-open'?" Karie inquired.

"You are not buying the calls, Karie," Max answered, "you are selling to someone the right to buy your shares at a specific price and over a specific time period. And this is the opening of the transaction for you, so it is referred to as 'sell-to-open,' or your broker may call it 'sell covered call.' If you decided later that you wanted to close out the transaction rather than wait for the options to expire or be exercised on the expiration date, you would then do the opposite and enter an order to 'buy-to-close.' That would close out the transaction. I hardly ever recommend doing that, as we'll discuss in more detail.

"I think I've got it," Karie responded.

"When you have entered your order, John or some other buyer buys your contracts through his broker and pays $3,000. The deal is settled and you get the money placed into your brokerage account *the next day*. You are free to immediately withdraw that money, let it sit, or invest it in something else that will also produce more income or gain opportunity!"

Ernie jumped in. "I just can hardly believe that you get your investment return up front...the day after you do the deal. Why, if you were buying a bank CD or a government or corporate bond, you would have to wait a long time before you would see any of your return."

"Well," responded Max, "that's just the way the creature works. The buyer obviously has to pay for the buy side of the transaction immediately, and you are the lucky beneficiary of immediate cash when you are on the sell side of the transaction!

"So what do you do after you have sold your calls? Almost always, you will just sit on them and wait for the expiration date to occur. We will discuss some other alternatives later, but mostly you will just wait it out until expiration. You can look forward to each passing day, as time is the best friend of an option writer. Every day that ticks off toward the expiration date means you are closer to the time you can either write a new option on your stock or you will receive cash for your stock at the strike price.

"Let's assume for a moment that the market price of KKK stock remains at $50 on the expiration date. What happens? Well, as we've said earlier, a buyer would not pay the higher strike price for a stock that he could buy at a lower price on the open market. So, the options expire unexercised. You have previously pocketed the buyer's $3,000 and you get to keep your stock. Now you can write more call options. With the stock price the same, if you write another one to expire in about the same time period later, you will likely receive a similar amount of option writing income as in the previous transaction. In fact, if you were to do that for an entire year and the price of KKK shares would remain at $50 at the end of the year, you would have received a return of over 17% from your premium income. An owner of KKK shares who did not write options would have no gain at all! How's that for a nice gain in a flat market?"

For Ernie the clouds just parted and the sun came out. "Now I see what you mean about option writing working its magic in a flat to slowly rising market." Karie also nodded affirmatively, grinning with similar enlightenment.

"Right! And if KKK shares closed above $55 on the June expiration date you would receive $55,000 and could then use the proceeds as you please. A serious option writer would probably buy more stock in some company on their working list of targeted stocks they would like to own and then write more option contracts. The cycle goes on and on."

"What if your KKK stock closed between $50 and $55…say $54?" Karie asked?

"You still get to keep all of your option premium *and* your KKK shares, as the price of the stock was still not above the $55 strike price on the expiration date. The nice thing about this is that you have kept your stock, but it is now worth more than when you wrote your option in January ($54 vs. $50). Not only do you have a gain in the stock, but when you write your next option contracts, say the September contract, you will find that the $55 strike price contracts will be trading at a higher relative price, adjusted for the difference in time to expiration…perhaps $4. This is because the market price is closer to the strike price now than it was the last time you wrote the option contracts. Remember that for out-of-the-money calls, the closer the market price is to the strike price, the higher the option  premium will be. This time your ten contracts would give you about $4,000 of premium income...and for even less time to expiration.

"Another strategy that might be effectively used in this case would be to write contracts at a higher strike price...for example the $60 contract instead of the $55 contract. This would reduce your premium income because the strike price is higher, but it would allow for more room for the price to increase in KKK stock by the next selected expiration date. The strike price you select will largely be based on what you think may happen to the stock price by the next selected expiration date. Of course, that is very difficult to know, but the investor usually has some informed thoughts on the subject from the research that's been done and the recommendation of the investment advisory service."

"That's all very positive stuff," Ernie said, "but what if the price of KKK stock went down?"

"That's when 'bad' is really 'not quite so bad,'" Max responded. We haven't talked about what the situation would be if KKK stock went down by the expiration date, so let's do that. Let's say at the June expiration KKK shares are trading at $48. You have the premium income of $3,000 to keep and obviously you get to keep your stock, because the buyer of the call would not pay you $55 per share for stock that could be bought on the open market for $48. Since you received $3 per share in premium income, you have a $1 net gain per share in the transaction from the date the contracts were written ($48 + $3 - $50). You have fared far better than a shareholder that simply owned the stock and did not write options on it. You have had $3 per share of downside protection, which is somewhat like insurance, during the entire term of the contract until expiration. Of course, if KKK stock went down even further than that, you could experience an overall loss, but a loss that would be less than if you hadn't written the option contracts.

"So what would you do then after the expiration of the options with your $48 KKK shares? There are several things you could do, depending on how you feel about the stock's prospects and what is going on in the market and the economy in general. These are your choices:

"If you believe your stock has significant near-term recovery potential:

(1)   Simply hold the stock and do not write options for awhile, allowing the stock to rise without it being called away.

or

(2)   Write calls that are further out-of-the-money…that is, write calls with a strike price that is significantly higher than the current market price. You won't get a huge premium, but you will get some. And the likelihood of your shares being called away is greatly reduced if the price of the stock goes up.

"If you believe your stock has significant further near-term loss potential:

(1)   Sell your stock now and wait for a better investment climate for this stock or another one.

or

(2)   Write calls that have a strike price that is only slightly above or perhaps even somewhat below the

current market price...the in-the-money option contracts. This will provide you with much better premium income and therefore a lot more downside protection. As we discussed earlier, I almost never recommend writing in-the-money calls, where the strike price is below the market price. If you are wrong and the price of the stock goes up, you will have your stock called away at a price that may not make you very happy. So, this is the only time that you should ever consider such a strategy...and be sure you really believe that your stock has a strong chance of declining in value below the strike price of your options.

"If you believe your stock's price will meander about where it is or go up a bit:

> Treat this as a normal option writing opportunity, because this is when option writing works its best magic. You may wish to write call contracts with a shorter-term expiration and also try to ratchet the strike prices up at expirations if the stock is gradually increasing in value so you get back to the position you were in originally.

"Remember...it is still possible to lose money buying stocks and writing call options if the price of your stock declines significantly. But if you are caught in a declining market where your shares are going down in price, you will *always* be better off if you have written calls on your shares compared with just owning the stock alone, because the premium income gives you the added downside price protection 'insurance.'

AN OPTION WRITER'S DREAM

"What would be the optimum situation for an option writer to maximize gain opportunities? This is difficult to achieve, but as an option writer you will have this happen to you on occasion to some degree or another with some of your shares. The optimum situation is to write calls so that on the expiration date the market value of the shares is just under the strike price. In addition to the premium income you keep your stock, so you can write new options at a higher strike price and continue to do this over and over again at each expiration date if the stock price keeps slowly rising. In this perfect world you would receive steady premium income, but by keeping your stock as it goes up to a price just below your strike price, your shares become increasingly worth more too.

"Let's give a highly embellished example. You buy JJJ shares at $50 and write contracts on them at a strike price of $55 and receive a premium of $3. On expiration your stock is trading at $54 ¾, so you write more options at a $60 strike price and receive $2 ½ in premium income. At the next expiration the stock is trading at $59 ½. You write more options at a $65 strike price, and this time you get $2 ¼ in premium income per share. One more time! At this expiration your stock is trading at $64, so you write the $70 strike price and get $2 in option premium income. At the expiration your stock is trading right at $70. How did you do? Well, you paid $50 for shares that are now worth $70. In addition, you have collected $9 ¾ in premium income. You total gain from start to finish is $29 ¾ per share. You are a genius…and you are way ahead of your colleagues who have only bought the stock and held onto it with a $20 per share gain. Of course, they have never had to worry about having their stock called away from them. But don't forget, you've had quite a bit of downside price protection too in case the shares started heading south, and a lot more predictability in your overall return as you collected all of those option premiums!"

Karie had a question. "Does it concern you when the prices of your stocks move above the strike price or when your shares get called away from you at expiration?"

"I don't really worry about having my shares called away from me. I am an investor who owns good common stocks and who achieves an above average return on a consistent basis by writing call option contract premiums on my shares. That's my game…that's the business I'm in as an investor…and I'm sticking to it! I'd be very happy if all the shares I write options on were called away from me at every option expiration date. That way I wouldn't have any losses and I'd be achieving my most optimistic objective, premium income, dividend income and capital appreciation too, every time. Between my premium income, dividends and capital appreciation, I'd be doing extremely well…returns way above twelve-percent and well beyond what Warren Buffett has achieved over the long haul, I'd dare say!"

"But isn't there a risk that you end up having all of your best performing stocks called away from you with only the losers remaining in your portfolio?" Ernie inquired.

"That's an interesting line of thought, Ernie," Max observed, "but that just isn't my experience. We've talked at some length about using an investment advisory service to be sure that you are selecting good quality stocks that have long-term growth potential. Whether you are writing call options or just buying stocks to hold, you should never buy a stock that you aren't comfortable holding for the long term. And you should never buy a stock just because it would give you a lot of premium income. That implies it's a volatile stock, meaning that it has a lot of downside potential in a bad market as it does upside potential in a good market.

"You also have to keep in mind that when you write call options you are talking about a rather short time horizon for the option. In most cases you won't be writing three-year LEAPS on your stocks that would provide a lot of time for the stock to go up significantly. You could write a long-term option in an isolated case for diversification of your expiration dates, but that would probably be the exception rather than the rule. For shorter-term options, there usually just isn't enough time for a stock to go way beyond the strike price, particularly if you leave some room for capital appreciation by writing out-of-the-money calls.

"That's not to say that it can't happen. It will, on occasion. Maybe some important, positive news will come out on a company you own and the price will spike upward suddenly. Of course, when the stock is called away from you, you can simply buy it back again and either hold it or write more calls on it. It will cost you more to buy it back the second time than it did the first time, but you will have the premium income to help too. On occasion you will find the opposite happen, where you have your stock called away from you and then the price goes down so that you can buy it back for less than the strike price at which it was earlier called away. Obviously there are a lot of different ways this can go.

"The most important thing is that you buy stocks that make you comfortable and you stick with them until there is a reason to sell them. That would usually mean that something has fundamentally changed with the business that makes you uncomfortable. If that happens, and the price of the stock has gone down, at least you have protected yourself somewhat by the premium income you have collected. And if some of your stock is called away, you should always ask yourself if you should buy the stock back again, or if there is another company on your working list that meets your criteria for investment."

"I guess the possibility of missing out on a good sized gain isn't too much of a price to pay when you consider all of the advantages that writing covered calls offers us in meeting our objectives," Ernie concluded.

"I believe that to be correct, Ernie," Max agreed.

"The hypothetical scenarios we've discussed won't happen to you in the way they were described. I've just included them for purposes of understanding what an optimum objective might be. But with common sense in your stock picking and the tools this program offers, you will soon find yourself well on your way to selecting option writing opportunities that will provide you with solid double-digit returns. Just imagine the cocktail party conversations you will have with your friends and acquaintances! I can assure you, the subject of covered call writing is not one that comes up often. It's not a 'secret'…but it is certainly not understood in any widespread manner by the investing public in general."

The Guru had delivered the philosophy of his covered call option writing program. Max could see that Ernie's and Karie's heads were spinning by now. They had covered a lot of material and the two of them needed time to take it all home, digest it and think about it before they continued.

"So there's the program. I think that's enough for today. Next time we'll get into the practical applications of all this to make it work for you. Do you have any questions before we close out for today?" Max asked.

"Frankly," Ernie responded, "I'm too overwhelmed at the moment. You certainly are a guru in every sense of the word, Max. I've taken some good notes. By next meeting, Karie and I will understand this so we can work with you to start applying it to our investments. Thanks…very much!"

"You are most welcome. How about a week from today for the next and most important installment?" Max asked.

"You've got it!" Karie responded quickly.

Max was prepared to assign a piece of homework. "I'll ask you to do one thing before we meet next week. Do you think you could decide on a list of stocks you would like to own for the long-term in your portfolio for option writing purposes?"

Ernie was ready for this one. "Actually, Max," Ernie responded, "we've begun that process. We have some stocks already that we really like for the long-term. And, we've been browsing through Zacks on the Internet. We've looked hard at the 'Brokerage Firm Buy List' and really like some of its selections. And ironically, a few of the stocks we already own are on that list. We'd like to work with that, at least to get started." 

"Fine," Max replied. "Just one more thing. So that we can get into specifics at our next meeting, would you please select, say, a half dozen stocks that you would like to use for figuring option returns? Then send those names to me and I will do some pre-work on them for our next meeting. We'll be ready to get started on it next Friday."

"Will do, Max," Ernie answered.

Ernie and Karie were tired and a bit numb from their session. Yet they sensed that The Guru's program gave them the best chance they could ever have to reach their twelve-percent goal if the predictions were true about slower growth stock markets. They left for home with a growing sense of excitement and enthusiasm to learn all they could about this investment opportunity which was so new to them.

PRACTICAL APPLICATIONS FOR MAKING MONEY

TIME VALUE AND INTRINSIC VALUE

Determine the time value and the intrinsic value of the following options:

Option Exp./Strike	Market Price of Under-lying Stock	Market Price of Option	Time Value	Intrinsic Value
AAA July $50	$52 ½	$4.00	$________	$________
BBB October $100	$93	$6.50	$________	$________
JJJ July $25 ½	$25 ½	$1.70	$________	$________

"CASE STUDIES"

a. Your cost for AAA stock is $55 per share. The current market value is $42 per share. You have collected $6 per share from two different option writing opportunities thus far. It's been a tough market, but things are starting to improve and you feel AAA's stock could get a nice bounce in the next six months. You have no option contracts currently on the stock.

What action would you take?

____

____

b. You just bought AAA stock at $44 per share. You are looking for option writing opportunities. It is your belief that there is not much downside risk in the market, but there is probably not much upside opportunity either in the near term. You are interested in maximizing income.

What action would you take?

____

____

c. You own AAA stock at a cost of $49 per share. About two months ago you wrote call contracts at a $50 strike price and received premium income of $3 per share. The options have now expired without being exercised, and the stock is now trading at $48 per share. You are concerned that the market will deteriorate over the next few months, and that your stock will follow suit.

What action would you take?

____

____

TIME VALUE AND INTRINSIC VALUE:
   AAA July $50: time value is $1 ½ ; intrinsic value is $2 ½
   BBB October $100: time value is $6 ½; intrinsic value is $0
   JJJ July $25 ½: time value is $1.70; intrinsic value is $0

"CASE STUDIES":
   a. If you felt strongly that the price of the stock would rise, you might not write new options until the price rise had occurred. Alternatively, you could write very short-term options at a higher strike price, say $50 or $55. The premium income would not be large, but there would be significant room for capital appreciation if the price does rise before the stock would be called away from you.
   b. With the opinion that the market would remain relatively flat, it would probably be best to write calls with a $45 strike price.
   c. If you believe strongly that the market price of your shares will decline, you should consider selling the stock. An alternative strategy would be to write the in-the-money $45 calls to maximize premium income and provide more downside protection, recognizing that if the market stays the same or increases your stock would likely be called away from you below your cost. You would have collected quite a bit of premium income, however, so that overall you may be in a profitable position.

DON'T FIGHT THE FED!

This well-known belief, attributed to noted investor Martin Zweig, seems to have been an investment truth in the past. It implies that during times when the Federal Reserve is increasing short-term interest rates (most notably the Fed funds rate) the market will surely go down. It also implies that when the Fed is cutting interest rates the market will inevitably go up. Has this belief seen its last legs?

Date	Fed Action	Resulting Fed Funds Rate	NASDAQ Closing Price
End of 2000		6 ½ %	2,471
Jan 3, 2001	cut rate by ½ %	6 %	2,617
Jan 31, 2001	cut rate by ½ %	5 ½ %	2,773
Mar 20, 2001	cut rate by ½ %	5 %	1,857
Apr 18, 2001	cut rate by ½ %	4 ½ %	2,079
May 15, 2001	cut rate by ½ %	4 %	2,086
Jun 27, 2001	cut rate by ¼ %	3 ¾%	2,075
Aug 21, 2001	cut rate by ¼ %	3 ½ %	1,831
Sep 17, 2001	cut rate by ½ %	3 %	1,580
Oct 2, 2001	cut rate by ½ %	2 ½ %	1,492
Nov 6, 2001	cut rate by ½ %	2 %	1,835
Dec 11, 2001	cut rate by ¼ %	1 ¾ %	1,950
Nov 6, 2002	cut rate by ½%	1 ¼ %	1,415

Since the Fed began cutting rates on January 3, 2001 through its last cut on November 6, 2002, the NASDAQ declined by about 43%. Look to see where it is now.

Perhaps the markets will recover from the burst of the Internet and telecom bubble and this investment "truth" will hold. Until then...there's another saying on Wall Street about buying stocks that's been heard more often of late: DON'T TRY TO CATCH A FALLING KNIFE!

Remember that writing covered calls can help provide downside protection

7

SELECTING OPTION ALTERNATIVES

> In theory, there is no difference between theory and practice. But, in practice, there is.
>
> Jan L.A. van de Snepscheut

Ernie and Karie wasted no time in selecting six stocks from their portfolio they had owned for the long-term and on which they wanted to write options. For any new selections, they began using the Zacks "Brokerage Firm Buy List" after doing more of their own independent research on them. Ernie wrote a message to Max outlining his thoughts and dropped it off to him early the following week. It read as follows:

Max - Karie and I have studied the notes from our last meeting with you and have talked everything over in detail. I think we are making a lot of progress, because it is all really starting to make sense now.

We are very anxious to see what ideas you have for writing options on some of the stocks we already own. Here are the six names you asked for:

> *AAA Medical (AAA)*
> *BBB Technologies (BBB)*
> *JJJ Energy (JJJ)*
> *KKK Industries (KKK)*
> *RRR Electronics (RRR)*
> *TTT Pharmaceuticals (TTT)*
>
> *We'll see you next Friday...and thanks for everything!*
>
> *Ernie*

When Max received Ernie's message and studied the names of the stocks he had listed, he was pleased to see that the names were diversified in terms of the type of industries represented. Max wanted to discuss the importance of diversification of stock ownership with Ernie and Karie. He also wanted to show them that the option returns an investor could expect vary quite a bit depending on the volatility of the underlying stocks (the magnitude of price swings). The list they had submitted to him would clearly demonstrate this.

Using the Microsoft® Excel spreadsheet program, Max had long ago devised a template that he used on a regular basis to help him make decisions on which call options to write for the stocks he owned. It provided a wealth of information to simplify decision-making and saved a lot of time in "crunching the numbers," although the same analysis could also be done manually. In preparation for his

next meeting with Ernie and Karie, he used t
the stocks for those names they had sent to hii
out two sheets and reviewed the data he had pi
first appeared as follows:

SAME STRIKE PRICE,
DIFFERENT OPTION EXPIRATION DATES

DATE-----> 6-Jul

CO. SYM.	# SHS.	SHARE PRICE	MARKET VALUE	D IV.	OPTION EXPIR.	STRIKE	DAYS	OPTION SYMBOL	PREM.	$ PREM. INC.	PREM. $ PER DAY	CONT. YIELD	TOTAL ANNUAL YIELD	MAX. CAP. APP.	ANNUAL YIELD W/ CAP. APP.
AAA	1,000	$57.16	$57,160	$0.00	17-Aug	$65.00	42	AAAHM	$0.90	$900	$21.43	1.57%	13.68%	$7,840	132.88%
AAA	1,000	$57.16	$57,160	$0.00	19-Oct	$65.00	105	AAAJM	$2.95	$2,950	$28.10	5.16%	17.94%	$7,840	65.62%
AAA	1,000	$57.16	$57,160	$0.00	18-Jan	$65.00	196	AAAAM	$5.35	$5,350	$27.30	9.36%	17.43%	$7,840	42.97%
BBB	3,000	$16.79	$50,370	$0.00	17-Aug	$20.00	42	BBBHD	$0.55	$1,650	$39.29	3.28%	28.47%	$9,630	194.62%
BBB	3,000	$16.79	$50,370	$0.00	19-Oct	$20.00	105	BBBJD	$1.30	$3,900	$37.14	7.74%	26.92%	$9,630	93.37%
BBB	3,000	$16.79	$50,370	$0.00	18-Jan	$20.00	196	BBBAD	$2.10	$6,300	$32.14	12.51%	23.29%	$9,630	58.90%
JJJ	1,200	$43.40	$52,080	$0.88	17-Aug	$45.00	42	JJJHI	$0.70	$840	$20.00	1.61%	16.04%	$1,920	48.08%
JJJ	1,200	$43.40	$52,080	$0.88	19-Oct	$45.00	105	JJJJI	$1.60	$1,920	$18.29	3.69%	14.84%	$1,920	27.66%
JJJ	1,200	$43.40	$52,080	$0.88	18-Jan	$45.00	196	JJJAI	$2.55	$3,060	$15.61	5.88%	12.97%	$1,920	19.83%
KKK	1,100	$46.89	$51,579	$0.64	17-Aug	$50.00	42	KKKHJ	$1.00	$1,100	$26.19	2.13%	19.90%	$3,421	77.54%
KKK	1,100	$46.89	$51,579	$0.64	21-Sep	$50.00	77	KKKIJ	$1.65	$1,815	$23.57	3.52%	18.05%	$3,421	49.49%
KKK	1,100	$46.89	$51,579	$0.64	21-Dec	$50.00	168	KKKLJ	$2.95	$3,245	$19.32	6.29%	15.03%	$3,421	29.44%
RRR	500	$106.50	$53,250	$0.56	17-Aug	$115.00	42	RRRHC	$2.35	$1,175	$27.98	2.21%	19.70%	$4,250	89.06%
RRR	500	$106.50	$53,250	$0.56	19-Oct	$115.00	105	RRRJC	$5.10	$2,550	$24.29	4.79%	17.17%	$4,250	44.92%
RRR	500	$106.50	$53,250	$0.56	18-Jan	$115.00	196	RRRAC	$8.20	$4,100	$20.92	7.70%	14.86%	$4,250	29.73%
TTT	1,000	$50.41	$50,410	$0.72	17-Aug	$52.50	42	TTTHX	$1.20	$1,200	$28.57	2.38%	22.12%	$2,090	58.15%
TTT	1,000	$50.41	$50,410	$0.72	19-Oct	$52.50	105	TTTJX	$2.00	$2,000	$19.05	3.97%	15.22%	$2,090	29.63%
TTT	1,000	$50.41	$50,410	$0.72	18-Jan	$52.50	196	TTTAX	$3.25	$3,250	$16.58	6.45%	13.43%	$2,090	21.16%

Taking the stocks Ernie and Karie had given him, Max had entered the appropriate data for each one. He had picked a strike price for each that would allow for some capital appreciation (out-of-the-money calls), and then he had selected three different expiration dates for each stock. Using this as a discussion tool, he wanted to point out some important facts regarding how returns vary depending on the expiration dates selected.

The second sheet appeared as follows:

SAME OPTION EXPIRATION DATE, DIFFERENT STRIKE PRICES

| DATE-------> | 6-Jul | | | | | | | | | | | | | | |

X	X	X			X	X	X		X	X					
CO. SYM.	# SHS.	SHARE PRICE	MARKET VALUE	DIV.	OPTION EXPIR.	STRIKE	DAYS	OPTION SYMBOL	PREM.	$ PREM. INC.	PREM. $ PER DAY	CONT. YIELD	TOTAL ANNUAL YIELD	MAX. CAP. APP.	ANNUAL YIELD W/ CAP. APP.
AAA	1,000	$57.16	$57,160	$0.00	18-Jan	$60.00	196	XAAAL	$7.35	$7,350	$37.50	12.86%	23.95%	$2,840	33.20%
AAA	1,000	$57.16	$57,160	$0.00	18-Jan	$65.00	196	XAAAM	$5.35	$5,350	$27.30	9.36%	17.43%	$7,840	42.97%
AAA	1,000	$57.16	$57,160	$0.00	18-Jan	$70.00	196	XAAAN	$3.70	$3,700	$18.88	6.47%	12.05%	$12,840	53.89%
BBB	3,000	$16.79	$50,370	$0.00	18-Jan	$20.00	196	BBBAD	$2.10	$6,300	$32.14	12.51%	23.29%	$9,630	58.90%
BBB	3,000	$16.79	$50,370	$0.00	18-Jan	$22.50	196	BBBAX	$1.45	$4,350	$22.19	8.64%	16.08%	$17,130	79.41%
BBB	3,000	$16.79	$50,370	$0.00	18-Jan	$25.00	196	BBBAE	$0.95	$2,850	$14.54	5.66%	10.54%	$24,630	101.60%
JJJ	1,200	$43.40	$52,080	$0.88	18-Jan	$45.00	196	JJJAI	$2.60	$3,120	$15.92	5.99%	13.18%	$1,920	20.05%
JJJ	1,200	$43.40	$52,080	$0.88	18-Jan	$47.50	196	JJJAW	$1.65	$1,980	$10.10	3.80%	9.11%	$4,920	26.70%
JJJ	1,200	$43.40	$52,080	$0.88	18-Jan	$50.00	196	JJJAJ	$1.00	$1,200	$6.12	2.30%	6.32%	$7,920	34.64%
KKK	1,100	$46.89	$51,579	$0.64	18-Jan	$50.00	196	WKKAJ	$3.25	$3,575	$18.24	6.93%	14.27%	$3,421	26.62%
KKK	1,100	$46.89	$51,579	$0.64	18-Jan	$53.38	196	WKKAX	$1.90	$2,090	$10.66	4.05%	8.91%	$7,134	34.67%
KKK	1,100	$46.89	$51,579	$0.64	18-Jan	$56.63	196	WKKAY	$1.05	$1,155	$5.89	2.24%	5.53%	$10,709	44.20%
RRR	500	$106.50	$53,250	$0.56	18-Jan	$110.00	196	RRRAB	$10.40	$5,200	$26.53	9.77%	18.71%	$1,750	24.83%
RRR	500	$106.50	$53,250	$0.56	18-Jan	$115.00	196	RRRAC	$8.20	$4,100	$20.92	7.70%	14.86%	$4,250	29.73%
RRR	500	$106.50	$53,250	$0.56	18-Jan	$120.00	196	RRRAD	$6.30	$3,150	$16.07	5.92%	11.54%	$6,750	35.15%
TTT	1,000	$50.41	$50,410	$0.72	18-Jan	$52.50	196	TTTAX	$3.25	$3,250	$16.58	6.45%	13.43%	$2,090	21.16%
TTT	1,000	$50.41	$50,410	$0.72	18-Jan	$55.00	196	TTTAK	$2.05	$2,050	$10.46	4.07%	9.00%	$4,590	25.96%
TTT	1,000	$50.41	$50,410	$0.72	18-Jan	$57.50	196	TTTAY	$1.30	$1,300	$6.63	2.58%	6.23%	$7,090	32.42%

In preparing this sheet Max had picked three different strike prices for each stock that would allow for an increasing amount of capital appreciation before the stock would be called away. Then he had selected just one common expiration date for each stock. On this sheet, Max wanted to demonstrate how returns vary depending on the strike prices selected.

These sheets would do nicely, so Max dropped them off to Ernie on Wednesday. He asked that Ernie and Karie take a look at them prior to their meeting, as they would be the basis for their next discussion. He particularly wanted them to focus on the "Total Annual Yield."

When Ernie and Karie arrived on Friday for the meeting they were full of enthusiasm. They had not understood everything on the two sheets that Max had given them, but they had certainly taken notice of the numbers under the "Total Annual Yield" columns and had commented to each other that many of these yields well exceeded their twelve-percent objective. All three of them were ready to get down to the task at hand again.

"As you can see," Max began, "what I did was to take the six stocks you suggested and work up some possible option writing opportunities based on actual quotes I obtained."

"By the way, Max," Karie interrupted courteously, "where do you get quotes on these options anyway?"

"You get them through the brokerage company you use," Max responded. "We will go into all of that in great detail, Karie, when we talk about brokerages and how to do the trading. For now, what's important for you to know is that these are real examples of options that were available and the market prices for them.

"I'd like to use these two sheets as an important learning tool, but, again, these are examples of actual trades that an investor might consider when the time comes to start writing options."

"Good," Ernie responded. "We noticed that in many cases the yields exceed our objective, so we're anxious to hear more!"

Max continued. "I'd like to start by going over these worksheets in detail, because you will use this same format over and over again in making your option writing decisions.

"Here we go," Max said, taking in a large breath. "It's important that you understand all of it, so we'll go into each part even if it seems obvious. I'm not trying to insult your intelligence...I just want to be thorough, OK?"

"My intelligence is always subject to question!" Ernie responded with a hearty laugh, "And it even deserves an insult now and then. Proceed."

"Very well, then." Max began his litany.

"See the row towards the top with the little 'x's? In any vertical column where there is an 'x,' that means you need to supply the information yourself. If there isn't an 'x' in a column, that means the information in that column is automatically calculated for you.

"Many of the columns are obvious. The first column is the company ticker symbol on the exchange where the stock is listed…the New York Stock Exchange or the NASDAQ generally. There are three rows for each symbol because I've made three different call writing calculations for each company. The next column is the number of shares you own and then the current market price of the stock. What I did here was to put down the number of shares that would approximate an investment ownership of about $50,000 in each stock for consistency. I rounded it to the nearest hundred shares, as an option contract always applies to one hundred shares of stock, also called a **'round lot.'** So each option contract covers one hundred shares, and you can't write options for an **'odd lot,'** which is less than one hundred shares."

"Does that mean that a person should have about $50,000 invested in each stock to make this work, Max?" Karie asked.

"Not necessarily, Karie," Max responded, "but I'm glad you asked that question, because that reminds me of something else very important that I wanted to talk about with both of you.

THE IMPORTANCE OF DIVERSIFICATION

"You've indicated that your investable assets will be pretty substantial at retirement, and I know that you've carefully accumulated that amount based on your own specific needs for retirement and your assumption that you would like about a twelve-percent return on your stock investments on an ongoing basis."

"Quite right," Ernie responded.

"In setting up your portfolio, it's very important that you be adequately diversified in your investments. That means a balance between stocks, bonds and cash and perhaps other investments too. We are not going to get into a long discussion here about asset allocation between these investment types and we aren't going to have a lot to say about relative risk in your investments either…for example, owning technology stocks vs. owning financial stocks, consumer durables, manufacturing stocks, and so on. I will give you a list of books and Web sites that you can use as a reference to assist you with such things if you need any guidance, but we are going to stick to our knitting here and limit our discussion to the subject of covered call options.

"I do, however, want to make just a few brief comments on these other subjects before we continue. First, it is important that your portfolio be balanced. However, I believe that stocks need to play an important role in everyone's long-term portfolio, regardless of a person's age.

"It is also very important that you have a reserve of cash to meet current, future and even unforeseen expenses and foreseeable expenses. The last thing you would ever want to do is to have to sell stocks in a down market to meet expenses. For that reason, you should have a reserve of cash on hand at all times. Whether that is equal to six months, one year or two years of your projected expenses, or some other number, is up to you. I just want to be sure I make the point that a cash reserve is vital.

"Finally, you need to make a determination on whether you need a fixed income component to your asset allocation, such as government or corporate bonds, preferred stocks or other fixed income investments. Writing covered calls does give you a lot more predictability in your income than simply owning stocks, however you may choose to have a percentage of your total assets in fixed income investments as well. Does all of this make sense?" Max asked.

"We've talked a lot about this over the years, Max, and I think we've got a good handle on what we need for the cash fund and will make a better determination regarding fixed income assets as we get closer to retirement," Ernie responded. "Based on our review so far, if we can achieve a long-term average total return of twelve-percent on our stock investments, when combined with income from cash and fixed income investments we should be in excellent shape."

"Good," Max indicated. "Naturally the amount you allocate to a cash reserve and fixed income investments will have an effect on how much ownership you have in common stocks and therefore how much option writing income you will have from them, so they all need to be factored into your retirement income projections.

"Now, Karie, back to your question about how much needs to be invested in each stock to write covered call options. As I said, a call option contract covers one hundred shares of stock, so you could theoretically just own one round lot of one hundred shares of stock and then write one covered call option contract on it. We haven't talked about brokerage commissions up to this point, and we are going to defer that discussion until we deal with the whole subject of brokerage accounts. But as a rule of thumb, it may sometimes not make sense to write less than five option contracts on a given trade so that your brokerage commission costs can be kept to a manageable level. This would be especially true when the option premium under consideration is small, as the commission would consume a greater portion of the premium income.

"So that means you would usually own at least five hundred shares of the underlying stock, because that would be five option contracts. If you own one thousand shares of the stock, you would write ten option contracts, which would give you even more commission cost efficiency. But in any event, generally try to own at least five hundred shares of a stock if you are going to write call options on them.

"As to your question about how much to invest in each stock," Max continued, "it's important that you not only diversify between assets classes, such as stocks, bonds and cash, but that you also diversify within your stock portfolio. In other words, as a retiree you wouldn't want to own mostly technology stocks even if you were an individual who was willing to assume a high degree of risk, because these stocks tend to be quite volatile. Even though they can have great upside potential, we all know what has happened to technology stocks and the NASDAQ and we've already agreed that you should lower your concentration in our company stock after Ernie retires.

"I'm a believer that a retirement portfolio of individual stocks should ultimately include up to twenty different companies, depending on the investor's own personal feelings about diversification and risk. This should provide adequate diversification...and the diversification should be across a wide variety of industry sectors. Twenty companies are a lot to follow, however it should be manageable by using your investment advisory services appropriately.

"I note in the names you gave me that they represent a diverse group of industries, which is very good: technology, energy, manufacturing/diversified businesses and healthcare. So, as part of your overall stock portfolio, you are off to a good start in your diversification efforts.

"If an investor has $1 million or more to invest and wants to own at least twenty different stocks, that implies that the investor might decide to place about $50,000 in each stock. You may decide to invest somewhat more or less in any given stock, but this would be on average. That's where I'm coming from in the numbers I've plugged into these sheets."

"Does that mean that if an investor doesn't have at least a million to invest the use of covered call options won't work well?" Ernie asked.

"No, Ernie, it doesn't mean that at all," Max responded. "Ideally the investor should have up to twenty different stocks for diversification. It would just mean that the amount invested in each stock would be less. And it would mean that the smaller investor would be writing fewer call contracts for each stock, which would tend to increase overall commission costs relative to investment assets. But it can still be very feasible. Also there are a lot of investors who are comfortable owning larger positions in far fewer than twenty stocks and who might want to write calls on their stock. And even though I am a strong advocate of broad diversification, an investor who feels differently and is willing to tolerate greater risk might feel very comfortable being in that position. It's an individual decision obviously.

"Nuff said, if you will pardon the pun?" asked Max.

"Cute!" responded Karie Nuff, "And yes, I get the message. How about you, Ernie?"

"Huh? Would you repeat that, Max?" Ernie frowned and then laughed. "Seriously, I understand your points and they are very well taken. It wouldn't hurt at all to have some reference books on these subjects, but Karie and I have had quite a bit of discussion about these very things. For example, we've talked about how we will invest the money I get from my pension plan when I take it in a lump sum and what we will do with the concentration I have in our company's stock."

"Excellent," responded Max. "Above all, be sure that the stocks you choose to hold or buy are stocks you would love to own for a long period of time. They should be steady growth or value stocks that have done well over the long haul and can be prudently held even if a market decline occurs. And most importantly, they should be stocks that you have researched and you understand the business they are in and are comfortable with their prospects. I am always amazed by those investors who buy something on a whim or a tip and don't really have any idea what business the companies are in or what their prospects really are.

"I think Peter Lynch, former manager of the Fidelity Magellan Fund, is right on target. He tells investors that in the long run, a portfolio of well-chosen stocks will always outperform a portfolio of bonds or a money-market account, but that in the long run, a portfolio of poorly chosen stocks won't outperform the money left under the mattress!" [9]

"Brilliant!" Ernie agreed readily.

"Now that we have that behind us we can get on with the sheets," Max continued.

CALCULATING COVERED CALL WRITING OPPORTUNITIES

Ernie and Karie focused their attention back on the worksheets.

"The market value column doesn't have an 'x,' so that means the calculation there is automatic if you have entered the other information. Next you would enter the annual dividend payment per share of stock. A lot of stocks these days don't pay any or only a small dividend, but whatever it is if you enter the annual dividends per share it will calculate them in with the other information to figure your total investment yields.

"The column on option expiration deserves more detailed discussion," Max continued. "We've briefly said that there are thousands of stocks on which you are able to write covered call options. For any given stock, there is typically a variety of option expiration dates to choose from. Let's just take an example that I was working on awhile back for Wal-Mart. In early February I was checking to see what was available, and what I found was that there were options available expiring in February, March, June, September, December, and the LEAPS the following January, and a year from that January...just a month shy of two years away. This

---

[9] Peter Lynch with John Rothchild, *Beating the Street* (New York: Simon & Schuster, 1993), 305.

gives investors quite a few choices to suit their own unique call option writing needs. We'll get into more detail in a bit on how we make those selections, but for now I just wanted you to know that you would normally have quite a selection to choose from in making your option writing decisions. For any given stock, there is an **'option cycle'** which means that generally there are options expiring on the same four months every year plus the current and the next following month. Some offer LEAPS as well. Not all stocks, however, offer this many months in their option cycle."

Karie had been looking hard at the first sheet and had a question. "Max, it would appear that not all stocks have the same option expiration dates available in their cycle. For example, KKK Industries has a contract expiring September 21, but TTT Pharmaceuticals does not, is that right?"

"Good observation!" Max noted. "You are quite right, Karie. I don't think we need to go into this in detail, but, as I said, each stock is assigned a cycle of option dates by the exchanges where the options are traded. Many of the option expiration dates that are available to you for option writing are based on the cycle assigned to each stock. So, as you have pointed out, at this time as you look into the future you could write options on KKK that expire in September, but not in October. Similarly, you could write options on TTT Pharmaceuticals that expire in October, but not September. This may sound confusing, but it is really quite simple to work with. There are three different cycles, and they are set like this." Max handed them a sheet showing the following:

Cycle 1:	January	April	July	October
Cycle 2:	February	May	August	November
Cycle 3:	March	June	September	December

"When we talk about brokerage accounts, we will go into detail about how you find out what option expiration dates are available to you and how you get quotes on them and other information to plug into these worksheets.

"One thing that is always true, however, is that all stocks on which options can be traded offer an expiration for the current month and the next month. So, the October options would not be available for KKK if it were only February. But when we are in the month of September, there will be a September and an October option for KKK...simply because there is always an option created with an expiration for the current and the following month. Does that compute?"

"So, then in May TTT Pharmaceuticals doesn't have a September call option, but when we are in August there will be one for September?" Karie asked.

"You've got it right!" Max responded.

"I'll explain this all to you later, Ernie," Karie said, as she flashed him a sly grin.

"The next column also deserves some extensive discussion...the strike price. The strike price is the part of the option contract that specifies the price at which the option buyer has the right to buy your stock up through the expiration date. As we discussed briefly before, when the market price of any given stock goes up and down, the exchange where the option contracts are traded will open up new strike prices if they have not already been opened previously. So if shares of JJJ Company have traded recently from a low of $30 per share to a high of $80, there would be strike prices offered at least in $5 increments from $30 through $80.

"As you know, what I typically recommend is to select strike prices above the price where the stock is currently trading...the out-of-the-money calls. That will hopefully insure receipt of an option premium that will fulfill your yield objective and also provide the opportunity for at least some capital appreciation if the stock goes up. We'll get more specific about strike price selection shortly. But for now just know that you should usually select two or more different strike prices above the current market value of the stock and put those numbers onto the worksheet with the other information to help determine which is the one that works best for you considering the rate of return, the capital appreciation potential and the time to expiration.

"The column titled 'Days,' which shows the number of days from the current date through the date of expiration, is automatically calculated. When you enter the option expiration date, the number of days from the current date is subtracted from the expiration date with the resulting number of days placed into this column. So, for example, for the BBB Technologies option expiring October 19 there are 105 days remaining from the date the worksheet was prepared through the expiration date, and so on.

"The option symbol is the next column. You get that information from the broker you are using. It can easily be retrieved online or by a phone call.

(Reader/Investor: It is possible to determine the option symbol for many options other than going to a broker. Please see "How to Determine the Symbol for an Option" in the Appendix.)

"Finally, you plug in the current quote for the option, which you will get from the broker as well. Don't pay any attention to the price of the last trade. That is already history and is very likely out of date. Sometimes there can be quite a bit of spread, or variance, between the 'bid' and 'ask' prices that are quoted for options. The bid price is what a buyer is currently bidding or willing to pay to buy the contract. The ask price is what a seller is currently asking or willing to sell the contract for. Actual trading will usually take place between those two figures. Generally what I do is to take the bid and ask prices, add them together and divide by two to get the approximate midpoint. So, if the bid is $1.10 and the ask is $1.50, I'd use the midpoint of $1.30, or perhaps even a little less for conservatism, and plug that figure into the worksheet under the 'Prem.' column. This is the premium per share that you could reasonably expect to receive if you placed an order, so it should be pretty valid for your calculation purposes.

"This is really starting to interest me!" Ernie jumped in. "I like the idea of collecting the premium income. And, the very next day after you do the trade."

"Yes. You will see the total premium income you would collect under the next column marked '$ Prem. Inc.' The commissions obviously vary from broker to broker, so your own template will be customized to accommodate the charges for your brokerage accounts.

"The next column, 'Prem. $ Per Day' is simply the premium income you would receive on a given transaction divided by the number of days from the current date to the expiration date. This information might not be important to all option writing investors, but I like to see it so I can compare it with other option writing opportunities. Just another comparison technique.

"Next is 'Contract Yield,' which gives you the immediate percentage return from the premium for this transaction only, and it is not annualized. In other words, it just tells you what percent return on your investment you would be getting right now. Again, another comparison technique.

"Now we are really getting to the heart of the matter. The next column, 'Total Annual Yield,' combines the dividend income and also the premium income for the transaction and calculates the *yield on an annualized basis*. It's annualized because we are used to thinking about our returns that way. For example, when you talk about the return you are seeking, namely twelve-percent, you are talking annually. You don't say I want a one-percent return per month, because we just don't think that way. So take the example of the BBB Technologies options expiring on October 19. What this means is that if you could continue to write the same option at the same premium price and with the same frequency...days to expiration...you would realize an annualized yield on your investment, based on its current value, of 26.92%, not including commissions. Do you see what I mean?"

Ernie responded this time. "Yes, I think so, but that would mean that at the October expiration date you would need to do the exact same deal again and again to get that precise yield, right? And obviously it isn't going to happen that way, because the price of the stock will change, and that means the price of the options in the future will change too."

"You are absolutely right, Ernie," Max answered. "But it is the best information we have at a given point in time, so that's why it's used. Obviously we can't predict where prices will be in the future, so we use the measurements we have now. That gives us the ability to compare one option opportunity with another in an 'apples to apples' manner.

"The next to the last column is the maximum capital appreciation that can be made on the transaction...that would be if the stock is called away. Let me explain, still using the example of the BBB Technologies options expiring in October. A writer sells 30 contracts of BBB Technologies on the 3,000 shares owned (30 times 100 = 3,000 shares) at a strike price of $20 per share. Since the price of the stock is $16.79, that leaves a possible additional appreciation of capital of $3.21 per share if the stock is selling for over $20 at the expiration date and is called away. Take $3.21 times 3,000 and you get $9,630, which is the number shown in that column. So then, if the stock is called away at expiration, the writer would have realized capital appreciation of $9,630 plus the premium income of $3,900...no dividend income, since BBB Technologies doesn't pay a dividend...for a total of $13,530. If you divide that figure by the market value of the BBB Technologies shares and then annualize the combined return, you get a whopping 93.37%!"

"Put it in our account!" Ernie bellowed, obviously liking the looks of that example.

"Now, Ernie, if you would say to me that doing this every 105 days, in the case of this option writing example, is extremely unlikely, I would absolutely agree with you. But, again, making this total return computation simply allows us to make comparisons with other option writing opportunities, and for that purpose it is of great value to us. All of the work we do with the template will be done at a particular slice in time, OK?"

"I understand what you are saying now, Max," Ernie responded.

"Are you comfortable with all this, Karie?" Max inquired.

"I think so," Karie indicated, "but if I have any problem with it when we get home I'll just ask Ernie to explain it to me!" Karie gave Ernie a poke in the side with her elbow and a quick wink.

"Here's a CD/ROM for you to use on your computer in the future. It contains the Excel template for your PC, a file named 'calls,' so that you can make these calculations for yourself now very easily." Max handed the CD to Karie, as he had learned that Karie was much more computer literate than Ernie. "You do have Excel on your PC, don't you?" Max inquired.

"Yes, we do. And thanks for the CD. I assure you we'll make good use of it," Karie said.

(For you, Reader/Investor, this file is on your CD and there is an instruction page in the Appendix outlining exactly what data to enter into the template to assess option opportunities and how to customize the template to fit your own brokerage commission schedule. Worksheets are included at the end of the book for use by those who are not using a computer. Though more laborious, with a pencil, calculator and a little patience, you would have access to exactly the same information as those who use the Excel template.)

"Well, now that we've discussed the data that goes into the sheet and what all of the columns mean, it's time to start talking option writing investment strategy. Are you both ready?"

"Lead on, McGuru!" Ernie urged.

THE OPTION WRITING STRATEGY

"We've discussed the subject of diversification and the fact that some stocks are riskier than others, which means their stock prices are more volatile. That volatility is reflected in call option prices too and the yield that an investor can expect from writing call options. For example, of the six stocks you've selected, you can see that the greatest annualized yield on this first sheet would be for the BBB Technologies August $20 calls. The premium you would receive for this transaction would give you an annualized return of 28.47%, which is well over twice your objective. An observer of this sheet might say, 'Gee, why should I buy these other stocks when I can get that kind of a return writing BBB Technologies options.' The answer is that BBB Technologies' stock has significantly more upward and downward price movements than the other shares, and balance is needed by buying as many as twenty different individual stocks, as we have said, and, in addition, buying the stock of companies in a variety of industries.

"What your overall objective should be is to take your twenty or so stocks and select option writing opportunities on them which will average out to an overall return of at least twelve-percent, because that's your objective. You will exceed that return in many cases, but in some you won't...especially if you try to leave room for significant additional capital appreciation. So, don't lose sight of the forest because of the trees. It's your *overall return* in a diversified, well-balanced stock portfolio that counts.

"By the way, one benchmark you can refer to that will give you an idea of how volatile your stock selections are is to look at its 'beta.' The beta assigned to a stock is an indication of how volatile it is relative to the entire market. Since a beta of 1.0 represents the volatility of the market as a whole, a beta of less than 1.0 means a given stock is less volatile and a beta of over 1.0 implies a more volatile, and therefore riskier stock. The further away from 1.0 the beta gets under and over, the less and more volatile a stock is compared with the overall market. For example, if the beta for BBB Technologies is 1.6, it means that BBB Technologies is 60% more volatile than the market. The beta for JJJ Energy, a stock whose price is much less volatile, is only .4, or less than half as volatile as the market in general. Looking at the beta will help an investor understand why the premiums, and therefore the yields, would typically be considerably higher for a stock with a high beta than one with a low beta. Information about betas can be retrieved from your online brokerage account. It should also be available through Zacks and Value Line, either online or on hard copy. By the way, stocks with a high beta tend to outperform in a bull market and underperform in a bear market.

"Let's begin by looking at the figures on the first worksheet and use these as a means of strategizing about approaches to call option writing. I've narrowed down the selection of option expirations to just three here and for only one strike price per stock, but you need to remember that there are many more choices than those.

DIFFERENT EXPIRATIONS

"Remember, there is always a call option for every optionable stock that expires in the month following the current month. Those are obviously the shortest-term options available, except for the current month, and

sometimes they are the best choice, especially in a rising market. If you select options that will expire in about one month, there isn't a whole lot of time between now and the expiration. If you leave room for at least a several point rise between the current stock price of a stock and the strike price of the call option, the chance is less that the price will rise above the strike price to where the options would be exercised and your stock called away from you. If there is, say, $4 between the current stock price and the strike price, the chance of the stock going up that much is a lot less for an option expiring in one month than it would be for one expiring in three months, six months or a year.

"There's a logical progression in the price of the call option premium as the length of the time to expiration increases. You can see in all of the examples on this sheet that as the days to expiration become greater, the premium per contract increases. This will always be the case. The reason is this. If you are comparing options with various expirations using the same strike price, it makes sense that if you were a buyer of a call option you would be willing to pay more for one expiring in October than you would for one expiring two months earlier in August. That's because with the October contract the buyer has two more months for the stock to possibly go up so he can profitably sell his option contract or exercise it at expiration.

"As the number of days increases to expiration, *the rate of increase* in the amount of the premium tends to slow down. This causes a lot of option writers to stick more to the shorter term writing opportunities. I generally agree with this, although an option writer should usually try to have diversification in the expiration dates written. Shorter-term call options won't give you as much downside protection, however, as longer-term calls. So, the proper selection is dependent on your beliefs about what the near-term future holds.

"As you can see, the premium for the BBB Technologies August call contract is a bit less than half that of the October contract. Yet the premium per day, the annual yield, and the annual yield with capital appreciation are all greater for the August contract. That is simply a function of the shorter time period until expiration. The same is true in comparing the October contract with the following January contract.

"Let me expand on this just a bit. Let's say you have just written an out-of-the-money covered call on a stock. And let's further say, just for purposes of making my point, that the price of the underlying stock remains exactly the same during the entire period until the option expires. One might expect that the price of the option would decline in a straight line progression over its life until it expires worthless on the expiration date...like this." Max drew a diagram for them.

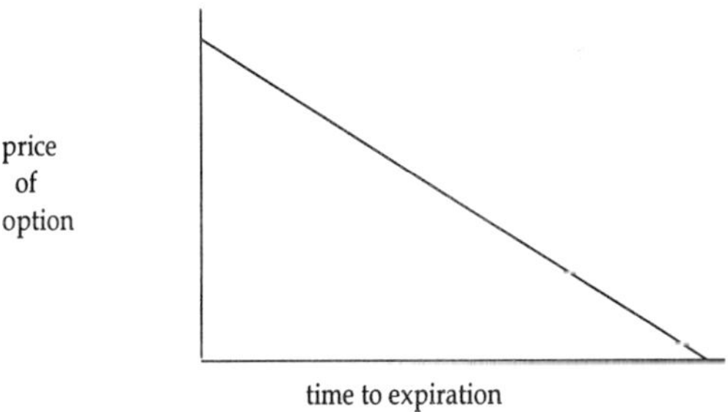

"That's not typically the way things work, however. Usually the time value of an option retains more of its value until it gets closer to the expiration date. Thus, if the stock price were to remain exactly the same, for a three month call option, for example, the decline in the price of the option as it gets closer and closer to the date of expiration might look something more like this." Max drew a second diagram.

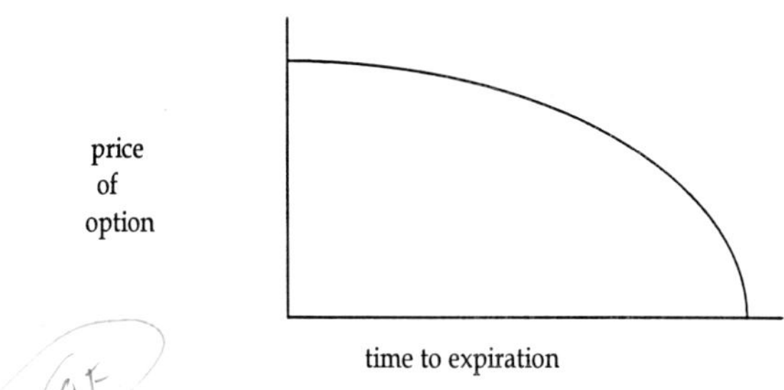

"As you can see, with a flat stock price the option holds more if its value until closer to expiration. An option writer could take some advantage of this by buying back calls to close just before expiration, say when the price of the option is only a small fraction of the original price when it was written. It wouldn't cost too much to buy them back at this time, and then the investor can write a new option at a higher premium with a longer time period to the next expiration than if the investor had simply waited for the first option to expire. The primary disadvantage of doing this is that the investor will pay additional commissions when the options are bought to close, which increases the overall cost. That's the reason why I almost always recommend holding the options until expiration. Some brokerages, however, reduce their commission costs quite a bit for option trades when the price on them is very low, which helps if you want to buy to close.

"What are the advantages of writing shorter-term covered calls and the advantages of writing longer-term covered calls? Let's do an assessment:

Advantages of writing shorter-term covered calls

- Less likelihood of your stock being called away from you at expiration because there is less time for the price to go up beyond the strike price.
- Greater yield on investment, given the time period of the transaction.
- Greater opportunity for more capital appreciation on the underlying stock, as you may be able to increase the strike price in future option writing opportunities if the stock price increases gradually.

Advantages of writing longer-term covered calls

- Larger total premium that will be available to you when credited to your account the next day.
- Less brokerage commissions, because you won't be writing new contracts as often if the expiration periods are longer. If you were writing only one month options, you would incur three times the brokerage commissions compared with writing options with three month expirations.
- More downside protection in the event of a decline in the price of the underlying stock since the premium is greater on longer-term options.
- Less administrative work, since you only have to research option writing opportunities, handle trades and do record keeping as often as options expire.
- Ability to do some tax planning by selecting options that expire in the next tax year (more on this later).

"So, given the advantages of each, what should a call writing investor do? Here the subject of diversification again comes into play. I believe the best strategy is to select a variety of expirations so that the options on your stocks are not all expiring at once or in large amounts. That spreads out your yields to help you achieve your overall return objective, but it does something else very important. Can you think of why you wouldn't want all of your options to expire on the same expiration date?"

Ernie scratched his head, and then figured it out. "I can think of a couple of reasons," he announced. "If the stock markets were in a broad decline at the time of the expirations, you would be faced with a situation where your stock prices were down a lot. You would have had some nice downside protection from the options that expired, but something tells me it could present some problems in writing your next set of options on your stocks."

"That's quite right, Ernie," Max agreed. "I'll demonstrate the problem with an exaggerated hypothetical example. Let's say you are diversified with twenty different stocks. Let's also say that the difference between the price per share of these stocks and the strike prices when you wrote your call options was a uniform $3 per share. That would have given you some pretty decent option writing income for the option period, regardless of when the expiration period is. The closer the market price of a stock is to the strike price when you write a call option, the higher the premium will be. Now, let's say that all of your stocks go down by $5 per share between the time you wrote your options and when the options expire. That means if you write a new set of options at the same strike prices you did before, the difference now between the market prices of your stocks and the strike prices of your new options will be $8 per share. That's quite a bit greater than the $3 the last time you wrote options. Do you know what that means?"

"The option premiums and yields you will receive this time will be a whole lot less than the time before that," Karie responded.

"Exactly!" Max said. "So, you would either have to accept much lower returns for that next option writing period, or you would have to reduce the strike prices when you write your next batch of contracts by $5 to give you a similar return. The problem with that is if the market starts to go up again significantly, your lower strike prices would mean that you would give up some of the upside appreciation in your stocks. They might be called away from you on the next expiration date at a strike price $5 per share lower than the strike price you used in the first option expiration."

Ernie jumped in again. "There's another reason you wouldn't want the same expiration on options for all of your stocks. If there was a broad rally in the market, you might get a lot of your stocks called away from you and be sitting with mostly cash at a time when the prices of stocks are a lot higher."

"Very true, Ernie. By diversifying into several different option expiration dates, it's a bit like buying a portfolio of diversified bonds with a variety of maturities, called a 'bond ladder,' so that you aren't faced with a large reinvestment situation at a time that may not be to your advantage.

"In fact," Max continued, "another diversification strategy would be to take shares in a single stock and sell calls with different strike prices or expiration dates. For example, with 3,000 shares of BBB Technologies, you might write fifteen contracts with an October expiration and fifteen with a January expiration using the same strike price. Or, you might write fifteen contracts with a $20 strike price and fifteen contracts with a $22 ½ strike price using the same expiration date.

"It just sounds like another way to broaden overall risk and reward exposure," Karie said. Max could see it was all sinking in.

DIFFERENT STRIKE PRICES

"You've got this down now," Max stated, "so let's go on to the second sheet. What I've done here is to keep all of the option writing opportunities with the very same expiration date...namely, next January, which is over a half-year away. And the reason I've done that is to demonstrate the effect of selecting different strike prices. In these examples, the total annual yield won't be as exciting. As you will remember, the longer the time to expiration the lower the yield, even though the actual premium you receive is larger with a later expiration.

"Let's take a look at the TTT Pharmaceuticals examples. The stock is trading at $50.41. The first strike selected is $52.50, which is the closest strike price available at this time above the current market price. The next higher one is $55 and then $57.50. We could select strike prices both higher and lower, but remember, we are trying to select opportunities that are both out-of-the-money and ones that will meet our overall objective of twelve-percent within our group of twenty or so stocks.

"Selecting from out-of-the-money options with the same expiration, the one that will always have the greatest premium and the highest total annual yield will be the one with a strike price closest to the market price...in this case the $52.50 strike price. You can see that at a premium of $3.25 it will provide a contract yield of 6.45%. Again, that's the actual yield of the option premium on this deal, but not annualized. Since we are looking at a little over a half-year to expiration, the contract yield is about half as large as the total annual yield of 13.43%. Note that this annual yield is above your objective.

"The next component to look at is the capital appreciation that can be realized if the stock goes up and what your overall yield will be if the stock is called away from you at maturity. For the $52.50 strike price, the maximum capital appreciation that can be realized is $2,090...the strike price per share of $52.50 minus the current market price of $50.41 times the number of shares, which is all figured into the sheet. Your capital appreciation can't be any more if you write the $52.50 strike price, since the stock will be called away from you at that price on expiration if the price is greater than that. If your stock is called away, the annual yield with the capital appreciation is 21.16%...well above the objective.

"So, as you look at a diversified portfolio of stocks and call option expirations, if you decide to write some calls with expirations as far out as six months, this particular stock and call option would suit your objective. It yields over twelve-percent based on the market price of the stock and the option today. It also gives you an opportunity for capital appreciation to get you to an annualized yield of over 21%. Of course, no one can know for sure what TTT Pharmaceuticals stock will trade for a half-year from now. Over time stocks tend to go up, so the odds may be fairly good that it will go up to $52.50 or above, in which case the

21+% projected return would be achieved. At least there's a greater chance of hitting the strike price with a half-year expiration than if you selected a one month call option, is that clear?"

"You bet," Karie responded. "Obviously it could go to $52.50 within one month, or one day for that matter, but the odds of it going to $52.50 in a half-year are much greater than it going to that price in one month, as the long-term bias for stocks is in an upward direction."

"Precisely, Karie," Max agreed. "In fact, TTT Pharmaceuticals' stock might very well grow by more than that by the time a half-year is up, as it often has done in the past. That's why in structuring an overall portfolio, an investor might look at a higher strike price, with the expectation that the value of the underlying stock could grow more, and also accepting a lower call option premium. Let's look at the next opportunity. The next higher strike price is $55. At a premium of $2.05 it offers a 4.07% contract yield, and a 9% total annual yield, which is under your objective. But the capital appreciation opportunity goes from $2,090 with the $52.50 strike price to $4,590 with the $55 strike price. So, if your stock were called away from you at $55 at the expiration, your annual yield including the capital appreciation would be 25.96%. To take this one step further, if you selected a strike price of $57.50, with a premium of $1.30 your contract yield would be 2.58% and the total annual yield would be 6.23%. But if your stock were called away from you at $57.50 on expiration, your capital appreciation would go up to $7,090 and the annual yield including the capital appreciation would be 32.42%.

"So, if you owned TTT Pharmaceuticals and were looking today at writing call options on it, what would your thinking process be in deciding what to do?"

"Well," Karie responded, "the first thing I would want to do was to be sure that such a long-term expiration fits into my overall plan for diversifying my call option portfolio."

"Yes," Max indicated. "You might well be selecting, say, one month, three month or even longer expiration dates as other alternatives. But in this case, we are just looking at the next January expirations, so what would the other considerations be?"

Ernie thought about it for a bit and then piped in. "I think the main thing to consider would be what you think will happen to TTT Pharmaceuticals' stock price in the next year. If you feel strongly that it has good appreciation potential, then you might opt for one of the higher strike prices to try to get the additional capital appreciation. As long as the total annual yield you select fits into the overall portfolio average of about twelve-percent, then maybe you shoot for the greater capital appreciation."

"But," Karie added, "if you really don't have a strong feeling about the stock going up, then it might be best to just get the higher premium, because that will give you more cash income up front and a bit more insurance toward the downside too. A bird in the hand is worth two in the bush, as they say!"

"Or," Max chimed in, "as Warren Buffett commented in his 2000 Berkshire Hathaway Annual Report, 'A girl in a convertible is worth five in the phonebook!'" [10]

Ernie and Karie chuckled. "You and Warren seem to have a similar sense of humor," Ernie announced.

---

[10] "Chairman's Letter," Berkshire Hathaway 200 Annual Report: 14

"Perhaps," Max said with a smile. "You are both quite right in assessing the considerations. Your decision must be balanced with the other things you are doing in your portfolio and with your outlook for each specific stock. For example, with a higher yield on BBB Technologies calls you might settle for a lower yield, and more capital appreciation opportunity, on the TTT Pharmaceuticals calls, but still reach an overall annualized yield of twelve- percent. Some option writers always go with the closest out-of-the-money option to maximize the option writing income. Others like a higher strike price to get more of a balance between option writing income and capital appreciation opportunity. There's no single best way for everyone. Both are good, depending on what your objectives and needs are...and your outlook for the specific stocks in your portfolio as well as economic conditions generally.

"As a general guideline, though, in assessing the relative attractiveness of option writing opportunities you should focus on the 'Total Annual Yield' column the most. This is the annualized return based on current dividends and premiums. The capital appreciation may or may not materialize, so don't get too starry eyed by the big percentages that appear in the last column.

"Just remember, you are in the business of achieving your return objective by call option writing. If your stocks were called away from you at every expiration, you might be missing some upside capital appreciation in certain cases, yet you would be meeting or exceeding your objective all the time, which is what you set out to do in the first place. That's the business you are in with your stock investments and option writing program...and you should stick to it!"

PRACTICAL APPLICATIONS FOR MAKING MONEY

PERSONAL "BUY LIST"

In addition to the individual stocks you may already own, start to develop your own "buy list" of potential stocks you may be interested in acquiring in the future. By using your research resources, including any investment advisory services to which you may subscribe, develop a list of three new stocks that you would consider for possible purchase and to use for covered call option writing opportunities. List the primary reasons why you have added these stocks to your "buy list."

Name of "Buy List" Addition:

____

Reasons for Addition:

____

____

Name of "Buy List" Addition:

____

Reasons for Addition:

____

____

Your life is a journey,

and it is about change, growth,

discovery, movement, transformation,

continuously expanding your vision

of what is possible,

stretching your mind,

learning to see clearly and deeply,

listening to your intuition,

taking courageous risks,

embracing challenges

along every step of the way.

NOT FOR THE FAINT OF HEART: HIGH RISK, HIGH RETURN POSSIBILITIES

> If you had your life to live
> over again, you'd need more
> money.
>
> Construction Digest

"Karie and Ernie, we've been talking up to now about the use of options in a way that would best suit you in your retirement. We've discussed diversification in your stocks by number…that is, hopefully working towards having up to twenty different stocks, diversification by industry, diversification in expiration dates of your options, and allowing for capital appreciation possibilities between the market prices for your stocks and the strike prices you select. We've talked about the fact that stocks with a higher beta have more price volatility and therefore command larger call option premiums than those with a lower beta. These stocks also have more risk.

OWNING AND WRITING CALLS
ON HIGH RISK STOCKS

"I don't know if you own any 'high risk/high reward' stocks at this time. If you do, it may not be appropriate for you to continue to own them after your retirement, or at least you might want to keep them at a level that doesn't exceed a small percentage of your total portfolio. I'm certainly not recommending that you buy any high-flyers just for call option writing, because the large call option premiums sometimes available on such stocks often don't outweigh the increased risk of owning the stock. But there are some pretty interesting returns a person can get writing call options on them if you own any. Do you have anything like that now?" Max inquired.

Karie responded. "When you told us about betas, I looked up the beta on each of our stocks. We have quite a bit of variation in the betas of the stocks we own now. Some of them are below 1.0, which you said means that they are less volatile than the market in general. Some of them are right about 1.0 and some of them are above it. We do own one stock with a really high beta...1,000 shares of Triple-O Internet Services, ticker symbol OOO. Its beta is a whopping 2.6! We bought it quite awhile ago after we heard about it online."

"It certainly has had a lot of volatility," Max responded, after quickly looking at the computer screen on his desk. "As of this time, Triple-O Internet Services has had a high of $63.25 and a low of $31.50 in the last year, and before that traded well above $100. It's right at $50 now. You probably purchased it with the idea that it might go up significantly in value, is that right?"

"Correct," Ernie responded. "And it did...but now it's back down around where we bought it. We should have sold...but we didn't."

"Well," Max continued, "I don't have a clue where that stock is going to go from here. There may be some room in your portfolio for high beta stocks like that going forward, but you will want to be cautious. Your objective is to get twelve-percent per year in total return. How confident are you that this stock meets your objective without too much downside risk?"

Karie answered thoughtfully. "We think it has the potential to go back up, but who knows when or if that will happen in this uncertain market."

"While we've been talking, I've put some numbers into our template. I'll print this out and show you." Max handed Karie and Ernie the following worksheet:

DATE-------> 6-Jul

| X | X | X | | X | X | X | | X | X | | | | | | |
CO. SYM.	# SHS.	SHARE PRICE	MARKET VALUE	DIV.	OPTION EXPIR.	STRIKE	DAYS	OPTION SYMBOL	PREM.	$ PREM. INC.	PREM. $ PER DAY	CONT. YIELD	TOTAL ANNUAL YIELD	MAX. CAP. APP.	ANNUAL YIELD W/ CAP. APP.
OOO	1,000	$50.00	$50,000	$0.00	17-Aug	$50.00	42	OOOHJ	$2.85	$2,850	$67.86	5.70%	49.54%	$0	49.54%
OOO	1,000	$50.00	$50,000	$0.00	19-Oct	$50.00	105	OOOJJ	$4.65	$4,650	$44.29	9.30%	32.33%	$0	32.33%
OOO	1,000	$50.00	$50,000	$0.00	18-Jan	$50.00	196	OOOAJ	$6.45	$6,450	$32.91	12.90%	24.02%	$0	24.02%
OOO	1,000	$50.00	$50,000	$0.00	18-Jan	$50.00	561	VOOAJ	$11.30	$11,300	$20.14	22.60%	14.70%	$0	14.70%
OOO	1,000	$50.00	$50,000	$0.00	17-Aug	$55.00	42	OOOHK	$0.95	$950	$22.62	1.90%	16.51%	$5,000	103.42%
OOO	1,000	$50.00	$50,000	$0.00	19-Oct	$55.00	105	OOOJK	$2.35	$2,350	$22.38	4.70%	16.34%	$5,000	51.10%
OOO	1,000	$50.00	$50,000	$0.00	18-Jan	$55.00	196	OOOAK	$4.10	$4,100	$20.92	8.20%	15.27%	$5,000	33.89%
OOO	1,000	$50.00	$50,000	$0.00	18-Jan	$55.00	561	VOOAK	$9.00	$9,000	$16.04	18.00%	11.71%	$5,000	18.22%
OOO	1,000	$50.00	$50,000	$0.00	17-Aug	$60.00	42	OOOHL	$0.25	$250	$5.95	0.50%	4.35%	$10,000	178.15%
OOO	1,000	$50.00	$50,000	$0.00	19-Oct	$60.00	105	OOOJL	$1.10	$1,100	$10.48	2.20%	7.65%	$10,000	77.17%
OOO	1,000	$50.00	$50,000	$0.00	18-Jan	$60.00	196	OOOAL	$2.45	$2,450	$12.50	4.90%	9.13%	$10,000	46.37%
OOO	1,000	$50.00	$50,000	$0.00	18-Jan	$60.00	561	VOOAL	$7.25	$7,250	$12.92	14.50%	9.43%	$10,000	22.45%

"Of course it could go back up quickly, " Max offered, "but here's one possibility to take advantage of some of that volatility we were talking about. Since high beta stocks have call options with high premiums, you would get a much higher total return by writing options on Triple-O Internet Services than you could with a lower beta stock.

"You can see here that there are some big returns that can be had by writing call options on this stock. If you write the $50 strike price, which is right at the current market price, you can get an annualized yield of over 49% on the very short-term option, to an annualized yield of almost 15% if you write the LEAPS expiring in about 1 ½ years.

"Even if you were to allow yourself quite a bit of extra room for capital appreciation by writing the $55 strike price option, your annualized yield would range from over 16% for the short-term call to almost 12% for the LEAPS. The LEAPS at a strike price of $50 would give you $11.30 per share of downside protection and put a total of well over $11,000 in your pocket immediately, which could be reinvested now to produce more option writing income. Of course, there's always the possibility that it could skyrocket and you would have been better off just holding the stock. That's the dilemma. I'm not suggesting that you write options on your Triple-O Internet Services. I just wanted to use this as an example of how high risk/high volatility stocks pay large call premiums to the option writer. But, even though this can give you considerable downside protection, it obviously doesn't fully protect you if the stock would tumble far downward."

Karie and Ernie were carefully looking at the sheet that Max had prepared. Both agreed they should take a hard look at the stock and obtain more research on Triple-O Internet Services before making a final decision on what action to take.

BUYING STOCKS ON MARGIN
AND WRITING COVERED CALLS
(DOUBLE YOUR PLEASURE
OR DOUBLE YOUR PAIN)

Max put his Triple-O Internet Services sheet away and continued. "As long as we are talking about higher risk strategies, there's one more I want to mention. I don't have any reason to believe that you would want to use it, but it's possible that there may be a time when your outlook for option writing is so favorable that you would consider leveraging yourself in order to get superior returns. This does not appear to be such a time now…and in retirement it may well never be appropriate for you."

"What is it?" Karie asked curiously.

"Buying stocks on **'margin,'**" Max replied. "Have you ever done that?"

Being in the banking business, Ernie was knowledgeable about margin accounts. At times Ernie had thought it might be opportune for them to buy stocks on margin, but he knew that Karie was quite conservative in her investment philosophy, so he had never felt comfortable in doing it. Ernie asked Max to explain how margin accounts work for Karie's benefit.

"A margin account is a brokerage account component that has been pre-approved by the brokerage through a margin agreement to permit an investor to purchase securities on credit and to borrow on securities already in the account. Interest is charged at favorable rates on any borrowed funds during the time that the loan is in effect."

Both Ernie and Max could see Karie was visibly twitching in her chair.

"I'll simplify this. When you buy on margin you buy stocks partially with your own money and partially with credit your broker provides. It's something like when you put a down payment on a house and then borrow the rest. Buying on margin generally allows you to buy up to twice as much stock with the amount of money you have than if you just used your funds alone. If all goes well, you would have twice as much gain by using margin than without it, less the interest cost. The other side of the coin is that if the stock goes down, you lose twice as much as you otherwise would have lost. So, there's both reward and risk. For people who are comfortable using debt to leverage stock investments, the relatively low rate of interest you pay on the loan to the broker can be earned many times over if the stock goes up and if you are regularly collecting option premiums. If it goes down, however, not only have you lost twice as much, but you are paying interest for the privilege.

"The further risk is that if the market goes down considerably, you would at some point get a **'margin call'** from the broker to add more money or securities to your account, or they would need to sell you out…most likely at a loss. Obviously you would not want to do this unless you have a pretty constructive stock market and option writing outlook going forward."

"I doubt that this is for us, Max," Ernie answered. "Especially going into retirement." Karie had an obvious look of relief on her face.

"I totally agree," said Max. "I just wanted to mention it to you as a part of our overall discussion. For investors willing to assume more risk, it may potentially fit into an option writing strategy. By borrowing on margin to buy stocks and then writing covered call options on twice as much stock, it is possible in a flat to rising market to earn substantially more on your investment than if you just invested with your own funds. If you were earning twelve-percent on your money, you would earn up to twice that by fully using a margin account, less the cost of interest on the amount of the loan of course.

"In a down market, it would be a disaster. Imagine someone who had bought Triple-O Internet Services at over $100 per share and used margin to double the investment. You wouldn't want to even think about the consequences of that!" Max said emphatically, rolling his eyes.

"High rollers we are not," Karie assured him, "…except, I guess, when we bought Triple-O Internet Services in the first place!" she said looking at Ernie with a smile.

"Let's call it a day, folks," Max suggested. "I think we made Karie a bit nervous with that discussion about buying stocks on margin."

"Well," Karie responded, "I guess when I think of taking risk I think of it not as 'risk versus potential reward,' but rather 'risk versus potential punishment.' In other words, in this case for me the glass is half empty and not half full!"

PRACTICAL APPLICATIONS FOR MAKING MONEY

List below all of the individual stocks you own (or are considering acquiring) and on which you will want to write covered calls. For each, list the current market price, your outlook for the stock over the next few months (price target, or more general statement regarding where you believe the price may head), the strike price you would likely use for call option writing if you were to write calls, and a month of expiration that might be preferable based upon your outlook for the stock and the relationship between the current market price and the strike price.

Company	Market Price	Outlook/ Target Price	Desired Strike Price	Desired Expiration
	$	$	$	
	$	$	$	
	$	$	$	
	$	$	$	
	$	$	$	
	$	$	$	
	$	$	$	
	$	$	$	
	$	$	$	
	$	$	$	
	$	$	$	
	$	$	$	
	$	$	$	
	$	$	$	

What is the diversification of your strike prices relative to the current market prices? What is your diversification of your desired expiration dates? If you own high beta stocks, be sure you know their financial potential to determine whether ownership of them plus the call option writing premiums you would receive can offset the losses that would be incurred if you are wrong.

DIVERSIFICATION WITH EXCHANGE TRADED FUNDS

Put all your eggs in one basket, and watch that basket.

Mark Twain

After agreeing to meet again the following Friday, Ernie and Karie promised to continue using Zacks and Value Line for more investment research and to play with the Excel template in order to get a better understanding of each of these resources. Max had also asked Ernie and Karie to bring their laptop computer and the Excel template with them to their next session.

As usual, Ernie and Karie were excited and ready for their next meeting with The Guru.

"Up to now," Max began, "we've limited our discussion to the importance of diversification in your stocks and overall investment portfolio and writing options on individual stocks. Until recently, if an investor wanted to write covered call options the only choice was to buy individual stocks and select the option writing opportunities. While that is still a primary strategy, it's now possible to get broad diversification with a single purchase of an asset known as an **'EXCHANGE TRADED FUND'** or simply **'ETF.'** An Exchange Traded Fund is bought through your broker just like an individual stock, although it has some characteristics of a mutual fund. They have a very low expense ratio charged by the managers of the fund to run the portfolio, generally ranging from about .18% to .84% currently. Unlike a mutual fund, however, ETFs can be bought on margin just like an individual stock."

"Thank you for pointing that out," Karie joked sarcastically.

"OK. Forget the margin part then," Max retorted with a grin. "An ETF owns a broad spectrum of common stocks designed to generally correspond to the price and yield performance of the underlying portfolio of securities. ETFs give investors the opportunity to buy or sell an entire portfolio of stocks in a single security, as easily as buying or selling a share of stock. For example, there is an ETF known as the FORTUNE 500® Index Tracking Stock traded on the NASDAQ. This fund tracks the Fortune 500 Index, so that if you buy shares in this fund you essentially own a small amount of each of the shares in this index. You can be assured that you are as diversified as this 500 stock index. These funds are a fairly recent innovation, and it's now possible to write options on a number of them. Some that you can write options on are:

FORTUNE 500® Index Tracking Stock (Ticker Symbol: FFF) – Based on the Fortune 500 Index™

Vanguard Total Stock Market Vipers (Ticker Symbol: VTI) – based on a portfolio of over 3,000 stocks

NASDAQ-100 Index Tracking Stock™ (Ticker Symbol: QQQ) – based on the NASDAQ-100 Index™ of 100 stocks

COVERED CALL WRITING DEMYSTIFIED

"There are well over one hundred ETFs, and options are offered on several dozen of them at this time. An investor can go to the American Stock Exchange's Web site, www.amex.com, and find a list of these ETFs and their ticker symbols. This can also be done on the NASDAQ's Web site, www.nasdaq.com. The symbols can then be looked up through your discount brokerage account to see if calls are offered on them.

"For now, buying the FORTUNE 500® Index Tracking Stock or the Vanguard Total Stock Market Vipers would give the broadest diversification while also offering the ability to write covered calls. For those willing to take more risk with potentially more reward...or is it punishment?...the NASDAQ-100 Index Tracking Stock™ is a possible choice. Its volatility is greater than the FFF or VTI, but less volatile than most individual NADAQ stocks would be.

"Here's one of our worksheets for each of these three Exchange Traded Funds that offer call options.

FORTUNE 500 INDEX TRACKING STOCK (FFF)

| DATE-----> 2-Oct | | | | | | | | | | | | | | |

CO. SYM.	# SHS.	SHARE PRICE	MARKET VALUE	DIV.	OPTION EXPIR.	STRIKE	DAYS	OPTION SYMBOL	PREM.	$ PREM. INC.	PREM. $ PER DAY	CONT. YIELD	TOTAL ANNUAL YIELD	MAX. CAP. APP.	ANNUAL YIELD W/ CAP. APP.
FFF	700	$75.70	$52,990		16-Nov	$80.00	45	FFFKP	$1.60	$1,120	$24.89	2.11%	17.14%	$3,010	63.22%
FFF	700	$75.70	$52,990		15-Feb	$80.00	136	FFFBP	$3.00	$2,766	$20.34	5.22%	14.00%	$3,010	29.25%
FFF	700	$75.70	$52,990		17-May	$80.00	227	FFFEP	$5.60	$3,920	$17.27	7.40%	11.89%	$3,010	21.03%
FFF	700	$75.70	$52,990		16-Nov	$85.00	45	FFFKQ	$0.40	$280	$6.22	0.53%	4.29%	$6,510	103.93%
FFF	700	$75.70	$52,990		15-Feb	$85.00	136	FFFBQ	$1.80	$1,260	$9.26	2.38%	6.38%	$6,510	39.35%
FFF	700	$75.70	$52,990		17-May	$85.00	227	FFFEQ	$3.75	$2,625	$11.56	4.95%	7.97%	$6,510	27.72%

"You'll note that the call option premium yields on the FFF and the VTI are not as great as they are on many individual stocks. These funds are portfolios of a large number of stocks. For that reason, if a beta were to be calculated for all of the stocks within the fund and averaged, it would be low relative to many individual stocks and would not be expected to experience the degree of volatility of individual stocks. As we've discussed, if the beta is lower, then option premiums will be lower as well...but so is the investor's risk. The broad diversification of the fund balances the risk.

"In the case of the FFF, the current market price of $75.70 is $4.30 below the next highest strike price of $80, which leaves some room for capital appreciation. At this time the VTI is trading at $94.75 with the next highest strike price of $95 being only $0.25 higher than the market price. Because of that, the option premium will be higher, and therefore the yield will be greater, but the opportunity for capital appreciation will be lower. Naturally the prices of these securities change by the second when trading is going on during normal business hours, so these figures are just a slice in time that will change constantly.

VANGUARD TOTAL STOCK MARKET VIPERS (VTI)

DATE------> 2-Oct															
X	X	X		X	X	X		X	X						
CO. SYM.	# SHS.	SHARE PRICE	MARKET VALUE	DIV.	OPTION EXPIR.	STRIKE	DAYS	OPTION SYMBOL	PREM.	$ PREM. INC.	PREM. $ PER DAY	CONT. YIELD	TOTAL ANNUAL YIELD	MAX. CAP. APP.	ANNUAL YIELD W/ CAP. APP.
VTI	500	$94.75	$47,375		16-Nov	$95.00	45	VTIKS	$3.45	$1,725	$38.33	3.64%	29.53%	$125	31.67%
VTI	500	$94.75	$47,375		21-Dec	$95.00	80	VTILS	$4.70	$2,350	$29.38	4.96%	22.63%	$125	23.84%
VTI	500	$94.75	$47,375		15-Mar	$95.00	164	VTICS	$6.50	$3,250	$19.82	6.86%	15.27%	$125	15.86%
VTI	500	$94.75	$47,375		16-Nov	$100.00	45	VTIKT	$1.40	$700	$15.56	1.48%	11.98%	$2,625	56.93%
VTI	500	$94.75	$47,375		21-Dec	$100.00	80	VTILT	$2.60	$1,300	$16.25	2.74%	12.52%	$2,625	37.80%
VTI	500	$94.75	$47,375		15-Mar	$100.00	164	VTICT	$4.05	$2,025	$12.35	4.27%	9.51%	$2,625	21.85%

"As you can see, it would be possible to achieve a twelve-percent return from premium income on a number of these strike prices and expiration dates. The funds also pay dividends to the extent that the stocks within the fund pay dividends, however the dividend payment amount and yield are not readily available to use in our calculations. The dividend payment rate would change with dividend increases or decreases in the individual stocks comprising the fund. Dividend payments would, of course, increase the overall return somewhat.

"The QQQ operates a bit differently than these other two ETFs.

NASDAQ-100 INDEX TRACKING STOCK (QQQ)

DATE----> 2-Oct

CO. SYM.	# SHS.	SHARE PRICE	MARKET VALUE	D IV.	OPTION EXPIR.	STRIKE	DAYS	OPTION SYMBOL	PREM.	$ PREM. INC.	PREM. $ PER DAY	CONT. YIELD	TOTAL ANNUAL YIELD	MAX. CAP. APP.	ANNUAL YIELD W/ CAP. APP.
QQQ	1,800	$28.82	$51,876		16-Nov	$29.00	45	QAVKC	$2.10	$3,780	$84.00	7.29%	59.10%	$324	64.17%
QQQ	1,800	$28.82	$51,876		16-Nov	$30.00	45	QAVKD	$1.65	$2,970	$66.00	5.73%	46.44%	$2,124	79.65%
QQQ	1,800	$28.82	$51,876		16-Nov	$31.00	45	QAVKE	$1.30	$2,340	$52.00	4.51%	36.59%	$3,924	97.94%
QQQ	1,800	$28.82	$51,876		16-Nov	$32.00	45	QAVKF	$0.95	$1,710	$38.00	3.30%	26.74%	$5,724	116.23%
QQQ	1,800	$28.82	$51,876		16-Nov	$33.00	45	QAVKG	$0.70	$1,260	$28.00	2.43%	19.70%	$7,524	137.34%
QQQ	1,800	$28.82	$51,876		16-Nov	$34.00	45	QAVKH	$0.50	$900	$20.00	1.73%	14.07%	$9,324	159.86%
QQQ	1,800	$28.82	$51,876		16-Nov	$35.00	45	QQQKI	$0.35	$630	$14.00	1.21%	9.85%	$11,124	183.78%
QQQ	1,800	$28.82	$51,876		16-Nov	$36.00	45	QQQKJ	$0.25	$450	$10.00	0.87%	7.04%	$12,924	209.11%
QQQ	1,800	$28.82	$51,876		16-Nov	$37.00	45	QQQKK	$0.20	$360	$8.00	0.69%	5.63%	$14,724	235.85%
QQQ	1,800	$28.82	$51,876		21-Dec	$29.00	80	QAVLC	$2.70	$4,860	$60.75	9.37%	42.74%	$324	45.59%
QQQ	1,800	$28.82	$51,876		21-Dec	$30.00	80	QAVLD	$2.20	$3,960	$49.50	7.63%	34.83%	$2,124	53.51%
QQQ	1,800	$28.82	$51,876		21-Dec	$31.00	80	QAVLE	$1.85	$3,330	$41.63	6.42%	29.29%	$3,924	63.80%
QQQ	1,800	$28.82	$51,876		21-Dec	$32.00	80	QAVLF	$1.50	$2,700	$33.75	5.20%	23.75%	$5,724	74.09%
QQQ	1,800	$28.82	$51,876		21-Dec	$33.00	80	QAVLG	$1.20	$2,160	$27.00	4.16%	19.00%	$7,524	85.17%
QQQ	1,800	$28.82	$51,876		21-Dec	$34.00	80	QAVLH	$0.95	$1,710	$21.38	3.30%	15.04%	$9,324	97.04%
QQQ	1,800	$28.82	$51,876		21-Dec	$35.00	80	QQQLI	$0.70	$1,260	$15.75	2.43%	11.08%	$11,124	108.92%
QQQ	1,800	$28.82	$51,876		21-Dec	$36.00	80	QQQLJ	$0.55	$990	$12.38	1.91%	8.71%	$12,924	122.37%
QQQ	1,800	$28.82	$51,876		21-Dec	$37.00	80	QQQLK	$0.40	$720	$9.00	1.39%	6.33%	$14,724	135.83%
QQQ	1,800	$28.82	$51,876		18-Jan	$29.00	108	QAVAC	$3.10	$5,580	$51.67	10.76%	36.35%	$324	38.46%
QQQ	1,800	$28.82	$51,876		18-Jan	$30.00	108	QAVAD	$2.60	$4,680	$43.33	9.02%	30.49%	$2,124	44.33%
QQQ	1,800	$28.82	$51,876		18-Jan	$31.00	108	QAVAE	$2.20	$3,960	$36.67	7.63%	25.80%	$3,924	51.36%
QQQ	1,800	$28.82	$51,876		18-Jan	$32.00	108	QAVAF	$1.85	$3,330	$30.83	6.42%	21.09%	$5,724	58.99%
QQQ	1,800	$28.82	$51,876		18-Jan	$33.00	108	QAVAG	$1.50	$2,700	$25.00	5.20%	17.59%	$7,524	66.61%
QQQ	1,800	$28.82	$51,876		18-Jan	$34.00	108	QAVAH	$1.25	$2,250	$20.83	4.34%	14.00%	$9,324	75.40%
QQQ	1,800	$28.82	$51,876		18-Jan	$35.00	108	QQQAI	$1.00	$1,800	$16.67	3.47%	11.73%	$11,124	84.20%
QQQ	1,800	$28.82	$51,876		18-Jan	$36.00	108	QQQAJ	$0.80	$1,440	$13.33	2.78%	9.38%	$12,924	93.58%
QQQ	1,800	$28.82	$51,876		18-Jan	$37.00	108	QQQAK	$0.65	$1,170	$10.83	2.26%	7.62%	$14,724	103.55%
QQQ	1,800	$28.82	$51,876		15-Mar	$29.00	164	QAVCC	$3.70	$6,660	$40.61	12.84%	28.57%	$324	29.96%
QQQ	1,800	$28.82	$51,876		15-Mar	$30.00	164	QAVCD	$3.20	$5,760	$35.12	11.10%	24.71%	$2,124	33.82%
QQQ	1,800	$28.82	$51,876		15-Mar	$31.00	164	QAVCE	$2.85	$5,130	$31.28	9.89%	22.01%	$3,924	38.84%
QQQ	1,800	$28.82	$51,876		15-Mar	$32.00	164	QAVCF	$2.45	$4,410	$26.89	8.50%	18.92%	$5,724	43.48%
QQQ	1,800	$28.82	$51,876		15-Mar	$33.00	164	QAVCG	$2.05	$3,690	$22.50	7.11%	15.83%	$7,524	48.11%
QQQ	1,800	$28.82	$51,876		15-Mar	$34.00	164	QAVCH	$1.80	$3,240	$19.76	6.25%	13.90%	$9,324	53.90%
QQQ	1,800	$28.82	$51,876		15-Mar	$35.00	164	QQQCI	$1.50	$2,700	$16.46	5.20%	11.58%	$11,124	59.31%
QQQ	1,800	$28.82	$51,876		15-Mar	$36.00	164	QQQCJ	$1.30	$2,340	$14.27	4.51%	10.04%	$12,924	65.49%
QQQ	1,800	$28.82	$51,876		15-Mar	$37.00	164	QQQCK	$1.10	$1,980	$12.07	3.82%	8.49%	$14,724	71.66%

As you can see, the strike prices are established in $1 increments, which is quite unusual. Therefore, with the current market at $28.82 per share, investors desiring to write covered calls that are out-of-the-money could select a strike price of $29, $30, $31, $32, $33, $34, $35, $36, $37…or even higher to suit their individual needs.

"A broad array of expiration dates are also available. Returns from options written on this fund tend to be quite a bit higher, even though it is a basket of stocks, since the stocks in it are largely technology oriented and therefore tend to be more speculative. If an investor is interested in technology, however, owning the QQQ would provide broader diversification than owning just a few individual technology stocks."

"By the way, you are also able to view a list of the top holdings for some of these funds, compare investment performance and request a prospectus online. Reviewing the holdings of the better performing funds might well give you some ideas for individual stocks to research further through your investment advisory service."

"These ETFs present an interesting alternative," Ernie said. "We may want to consider trying out one or two of them when we have some excess cash."

"They are an excellent investment vehicle to use for **'dollar cost averaging,'** in one-hundred share lots" Max said. "Rather than buying all of your shares at one time, an investor can spread risk by purchasing some of an ETF now and more later. It's always difficult if not impossible to know when to buy to get the best price. By dollar cost averaging, if it goes down, more shares will be purchased for less money. Dollar cost averaging is a good way to spread risk with the purchase of any security."

"What I like about these ETFs," Karie chimed in, "is that they appear to make diversification and covered call writing available for virtually all investors, even those with smaller amounts of money to invest. It's good that everyone can have an opportunity to use your program to their advantage."

"You are quite right, Karie," agreed Max. "And in the future there will be many more of these very diversified funds created based upon the broad market, industry sectors, size, region, investment style and international. No doubt an increasing number will offer the ability to write options. The covered call writing program is now feasible for most investors. In addition to being traded on NASDAQ, many of the ETFs are now being traded on the New York Stock Exchange as well."

PRACTICAL APPLICATIONS FOR MAKING MONEY

RESEARCHING EXCHANGE TRADED FUNDS

Go the Web site www.amex.com and check out some of the Exchange Traded Funds to see if one or more of them may suit your investment objectives. Note that there is a form on the site for ordering prospectuses for the ETFs offered. Remember, not all ETFs offer the opportunity for writing covered calls. Add the names of interesting ETFs to your "buy list" developed at the end of Chapter 7 for future acquisition and covered call writing opportunities. ETFs on which call options cannot be written today may well offer them in the future.

If you are not connected to the Internet, consider calling the toll free number 1-800-THE-AMEX for more information and to order prospectuses for ETFs.

DIVERSIFICATION OF INDIVIDUAL STOCK PORTFOLIO

List all of the individual stocks below that you currently own. Then list the industry sector in which each company belongs (e.g., basic materials, consumer cyclicals, defense, energy, financial, food and beverage, healthcare, technology, and any others which you wish to segregate). Calculate the percentage of each sector represented in your entire individual stock portfolio.

Stock Name	Market Value	Industry Sector
__________	$__________	__________
__________	$__________	__________
__________	$__________	__________
__________	$__________	__________
__________	$__________	__________
__________	$__________	__________
__________	$__________	__________
__________	$__________	__________
__________	$__________	__________
__________	$__________	__________
__________	$__________	__________
__________	$__________	__________

Sector	Market Value	% of Portfolio
Total Portfolio	$__________	100%
Basic Materials	$__________	__________%
Consumer Cyclicals	$__________	__________%
Defense	$__________	__________%
Energy	$__________	__________%
Financial	$__________	__________%
Food & Beverage	$__________	__________%
Healthcare	$__________	__________%
Technology	$__________	__________%
__________	$__________	__________%
__________	$__________	__________%
__________	$__________	__________%
__________	$__________	__________%

Based on this data, are you comfortable that your portfolio of individual stocks is adequately diversified?

WHY IT PAYS TO PERSIST
IN YOUR GOALS AND IDEAS
DESPITE NAYSAYERS AND DOUBTERS

"The telephone has too many shortcomings to be seriously considered as a means of communication." (Western Union internal memo, 1876)

"There is no reason anyone would want a computer in their home." (Kenneth Olson, president and chairman, Digital Equipment Corporation, 1977)

"The concept is interesting and well-formed, but in order to earn better than a grade of 'C,' the idea must be feasible." (A Yale management professor in response to Fred Smith's proposing a reliable overnight delivery service. Mr. Smith later founded Federal Express.)

"If I had thought about it, I wouldn't have done the experiment. The literature was full of examples that said you can't do this." (Spencer Silver on the work that led to the adhesives used on 3M's Post-It notepads.)

ALL ABOUT BROKERAGE ACCOUNTS AND WRITING CALL OPTIONS

> Education is a progressive discovery of our own ignorance.
>
> Will Durant

With the discussion completed on individual stock portfolio choices, Exchange Traded Funds, and selection of call writing opportunities, it was now time to delve into the mechanics of how to make it all happen.

ONLINE DISCOUNT BROKERAGES

"If I recall correctly," Max said, "you two are pretty comfortable using your computer online, and I know you already have a discount brokerage account. Do you do any of your trading online now?"

"Yes," Karie responded. "We've had both a personal account and a Rollover IRA account with a discount broker for several years. A year or so ago we started doing our stock trading online with them. We take our laptop with us on trips so we can trade online anywhere." Karie held up their sleek looking black laptop computer that she had brought to the meeting.

(Reader/Investor: In the event you do not have a computer and/or do not have an Internet access you will still be able to implement the strategies in this book. Please refer to the sections in the Appendix titled "How to Use a Discount Broker Without a Computer and Calculating Covered Call Writing Opportunities Manually" and "How to Manually Track Your Option Writing Transactions." It is more work than using a computer, but will become much easier with practice.)

"So, how has online trading worked for you?" Max inquired.

"Quite well," Ernie indicated. "Obviously we like the lower fees charged by a discount broker, especially the even lower commissions when we trade online. And it's so easy to do business that way. Also, having a cash management account where we can park all of our investments, including uninvested cash, is very simple and efficient. I assume we can use our online account to trade call options too, right?"

"Absolutely," Max responded. "In fact, you need to do your options trading with the brokerage where you have your stocks. And once you get the hang of it, trading call options online is much quicker, easier and less expensive than dealing with humans! You really won't have any need to work with an individual unless you have some kind of problem with your account."

"That's pretty much the mode we are in right now," Karie said. "I'm curious about what the brokerages charge to execute options trades."

COMMISSIONS

"There's a great deal of variance between these charges," Max told her. "The discount brokers generally charge far less than full-service brokerages, but even among the discounters there's a lot of difference. Most of all you want to be sure you are dealing with a substantial brokerage company who will be around for at least as long as you are.

"Typically discount brokerages charge for option trades based upon two components. First, there is usually a flat fee per transaction. This is why it is more cost efficient when you trade a larger number of call contracts, as this component doesn't change regardless of how many contracts are traded. Second, there is usually also a fee per option contract as well. This component tends to make it more expensive to trade a large number of option contracts on a lower priced stock or with a small premium.

"These two components are added together and charged as one fee per trade. As an example, let's say there is a $20 flat fee plus $1.75 per contract. If an investor sells 10 calls on a stock, the commission would be $37.50. The larger the number of contracts traded, the smaller the commission as a percentage of the premium collected. If you write about ten contracts per trade, you are achieving quite good efficiency.

"You can see that the way this fee schedule is structured, the commission does not vary with the amount of the premium collected. Therefore a commission schedule with a flat fee and per contract charge would tend to favor longer-term call options, as they will always have a larger premium per contract than a shorter-term option.

"For example, let's look at what the commission situation would be if you wrote call option contracts on from 100 to 2,000 shares of a stock using this commission schedule...that would be from one to twenty contracts. We'll look at it two ways...with a $1 premium per contract and with a $3 premium per contract."

Max reached into a file, pulled out a sheet of paper containing the following information and handed it to Ernie and Karie.

	$1 PREMIUM				$3 PREMIUM		
# CONT.	PREM. INCOME	COMM.	COMM. %	# CONT.	PREM. INCOME	COMM.	COMM. %
1	$100	21.75	21.75%	1	$300	21.75	7.25%
2	$200	23.50	11.75%	2	$600	23.50	3.92%
3	$300	25.25	8.42%	3	$900	25.25	2.81%
4	$400	27.00	6.75%	4	$1,200	27.00	2.25%
5	$500	28.75	5.75%	5	$1,500	28.75	1.92%
6	$600	30.50	5.08%	6	$1,800	30.50	1.69%
7	$700	32.25	4.61%	7	$2,100	32.25	1.54%
8	$800	34.00	4.25%	8	$2,400	34.00	1.42%
9	$900	35.75	3.97%	9	$2,700	35.75	1.32%
10	$1,000	37.50	3.75%	10	$3,000	37.50	1.25%
11	$1,100	39.25	3.57%	11	$3,300	39.25	1.19%
12	$1,200	41.00	3.42%	12	$3,600	41.00	1.14%
13	$1,300	42.75	3.29%	13	$3,900	42.75	1.10%
14	$1,400	44.50	3.18%	14	$4,200	44.50	1.06%
15	$1,500	46.25	3.08%	15	$4,500	46.25	1.03%
16	$1,600	48.00	3.00%	16	$4,800	48.00	1.00%
17	$1,700	49.75	2.93%	17	$5,100	49.75	0.98%
18	$1,800	51.50	2.86%	18	$5,400	51.50	0.95%
19	$1,900	53.25	2.80%	19	$5,700	53.25	0.93%
20	$2,000	55.00	2.75%	20	$6,000	55.00	0.92%

"You can see that the commissions paid are the same for both the $1 premium per contract and the $3 premium per contract. But the commission paid as a percentage of the premium income collected is only one-third as much for the options with a $3 premium as for those with a $1 premium.

"Also, obviously longer-term options expire less frequently. A writer of options expiring in one month would need to trade three times more frequently than a writer of options expiring in three months. So, you pay a lesser percentage of the premium income in commissions by writing call options with longer-term expiration dates. Of course, the commissions paid is just one of many factors you would take into consideration as part of your overall option writing strategy.

"Commissions on option trades tend to be higher than the discount brokerage commissions charged for a stock purchase or sale, which often run between $10 and $30, depending on the broker. But in recent years, fees on options trades have come down significantly and represent only a very small percentage of the call option writing income you will be collecting. And you will become a very important client to your broker. As you write more and more call option contracts, they will collect more fee income from you than if you were just the casual stock trader. It should be a win/win situation for both you and the brokerage. You may be in a position to ask them for a favor or special service now and then. Maybe they will even give you a free trade on occasion!"

"That sounds reasonable. So you feel we are in good shape with our present discount brokerage account?" Karie asked.

"Yes, you are," Max responded. "There are many online brokers such as Accutrade, Ameritrade, Harris Direct, E-Trade, Scottrade, TD Waterhouse, and on and on. I tend to think of Fidelity Investments and Charles Schwab & Company first. I am the most familiar with those two and they are among the largest and most financially sound. The commissions are higher with Schwab and Fidelity than with some of the other online brokers, but they are much, much lower than traditional full-service brokers. They both offer a full-blown cash management account at no extra charge and they pay a market rate of interest on uninvested cash balances. An investor should be able to go to the Web site of any of the online brokerages and check out the fees for stock and option trades very easily. Or, a phone call could be made to get the same information.

"By the way, the 'calls' template I've given you can be easily customized to include all stock and option fees charged by your brokerage in the return calculations. Just follow the instructions for use of the template and your calculations will be exact."

"Can we write covered calls in both our personal and our Rollover IRA accounts?" Ernie asked.

"You bet! There's no difference between the two when it comes to eligibility for covered call writing, as long as you are approved for option writing in both accounts by your brokerage.

"Shall we proceed with our discussion on writing call options online and assume that you will continue to work with your present online discount broker?" Max inquired.

"Yes. Let's do it. We are ready," Karie responded eagerly.

"OK. There are two things we want to focus on. The first is getting the information you need to complete the Excel template so you can make your decisions on what calls to write. Second, we want to talk about the process of executing the option transactions. The rest of it takes care of itself," Max said.

"So when we write covered calls our broker will automatically credit the cash to our brokerage account the next day? Do I understand that correctly?" Ernie asked.

"That's exactly right, Ernie," Max said. "All of the mechanics occur automatically. Not only will the cash be put into your brokerage account the next day, but with a cash management account, such as the one you have, they will automatically invest the cash in the money market fund you have selected for your account. That way your premium income is earning interest until you decide to withdraw it or to reinvest it in something else.

"And, if you have a margin loan balance, the money credited to your account from the premium income would automatically reduce the loan balance," Max added.

"Ain't gonna happen!" Karie said with finality.

"Right. I'm just covering all of the bases, Karie," Max reported with a grin.

THE OPTION AGREEMENT

"Before we get to the two key points, there is one critical piece of paperwork that will need to be completed before any option writing can be done. You need to sign an **'Option Agreement'** for each account you have with your brokerage so that you can trade covered call options. What you need to do is to call or write them, tell them that you want to write covered calls in your accounts, and ask them to send you the necessary paperwork to set up your accounts for options. They will send the Option Agreement form to fill out and also a publication they are required to provide called *Characteristics and Risks of Standardized Options*. This is a very informative booklet that reviews options terminology and theory, tells about the different kinds of options, how they can be used and the relative risks. As we've said before, some option strategies involve high risk and some, like covered call writing, are very conservative. This booklet reviews it all."

"Why is it necessary to sign an Option Agreement?" Karie asked.

"The purpose of the agreement is to help the brokerage assure that the investor has adequate knowledge about investing in options and that the option transactions are suitable for the investor. By the time we finish our discussion, you will be very knowledgeable about writing covered calls. But you should go ahead and request this now to get the account set up so you are ready.

"The Option Agreement covers a wide variety of option strategies, so when you complete the paperwork you should only indicate that you want to write covered call options. You will also be asked about your investment knowledge and activity, and you should answer those questions honestly.

"Finally, you will be asked about your investment objectives on the agreement. You should answer that you desire to produce income, which is consistent with writing covered calls.

"Once you see the paperwork you'll find it easy to complete. Just answer the questions as we've discussed and return it to your broker. It should be approved in a few days and you will be ready to initiate trades."

"I've made some notes to do this," Karie indicated.

"If that's clear, then, we'll hit the first point, which is getting the information you need to make informed option writing decisions.

"Let's get out the template printout with your six stocks on it and the option writing opportunities. I'd like you to turn on your computer now and bring up the Excel template I gave you for options calculations. We'll talk about how to get the information you need from your broker's online Web site.

COMPLETING THE WORKSHEET DATA

"As you know, you need to fill in all of the columns that have an 'x' at the top. You are already familiar with obtaining a lot of this information since you've been doing some stock trading online. Once you log on to your brokerage account, you can find out the ticker symbol for any stock. I'm sure you probably would do that by clicking on the quote section of their Web page and then entering the name of the company. I think I'm pretty safe in saying that the process is similar with Fidelity, Schwab and other online brokers. A little looking around for the right place to point and click should get you where you want to be. Of course, if there are any problems finding what you need, you can always call the brokerage company directly and ask them a few questions until you are familiar with the process. After that it will become very automatic, because you will be using their Web pages frequently.

"After you have entered the company name, ticker symbol, the number of shares and the dividend rate onto the Excel template, you are ready to get into the option writing part. By the way, you should be able to get information about a stock's beta using your access to research information online as well. Many of the online brokerages provide research through First Call, Standard & Poors, Argus and others that will provide this and other valuable research information.

"If you scroll to the right of the brokerage commission schedule columns on the Excel template you will see a progressive list of monthly option expiration dates. You should select the dates you want, one at a time, by placing your cursor over the first date, pressing the 'Copy' button, and then placing the cursor in the appropriate cell under the 'Option Expiration' column. Then press the 'Paste' button and the date will be there. You should do that on a separate line for each option expiration date you want to consider.

Then you need to type in the strike price you wish to review. Remember, you will almost always want to be working with call options that have a strike price somewhat above the current market price of your stocks. You may need to create some more rows and replicate the information for the same stock if you have a lot of expiration dates and strike prices you want to consider.

"Once you have this information in the template, you are ready to begin looking up quotes. This may be done a bit differently with various online brokerages, but typically what you do is request a quote on the stock by typing in the ticker symbol for the underlying stock. When you have the stock quote, you can then enter the current price information on the template in the appropriate column so it is up to date. When you are getting a quote on the stock, you should find the words **'option chain'** somewhere near the quote. By clicking on this, their system should take you to a listing of all of the expiration dates and strike prices offered for the stock. By scrolling up and down, you should be able to see the option ticker symbol for each option you wish to consider. As you scroll by them, note the ticker symbol for those you want and type in that information in the correct cell on the Excel template. Again, if it isn't obvious after a little searching how to find this, a call to the customer service center should get you the information you need.

"After you have gotten this information for a given stock and the call option you've selected, your row should be filled up to the premium column on the template. Now it's time to get the premium quotes on the option symbols and enter that information. By entering the option ticker symbol into the broker's online quotation inquiry system, the system should give you a number of pieces of information about the quote you are looking for.

"Most importantly, it should give you the current bid and ask prices. That is even more important that the last price at which the option has traded. It may have been some time since the last option trade, and the underlying stock has probably gone up or down. This would mean that the bid and ask for the option has also gone up or down, sometimes causing the last trade price to be out of date. Generally, when you are looking to do a trade on a call option, you can expect to make your trade at about the midpoint between the bid and ask, or perhaps a little bit closer toward the bid side. As I mentioned before, I would suggest that you add the bid and ask together, divide by two, and then place the resulting amount, or perhaps even slightly less, as the number in the premium column on the template.

"After entering the option price, the rest of the data will complete itself automatically. By entering the quotes in this way for each option symbol onto the template, you are then in a position to take a look at the worksheet and make a decision on what option you wish to write.

"So, that's how you use your online quotation system to obtain the information you need to complete your template. Gathering all of this data may take some time initially, but I assure you it will go quickly and smoothly after you have done it a few times.

"I won't go into the decision making process again, as we discussed it in detail earlier. Of course your goal is to achieve your total return objective while obtaining diversity in your option expiration dates and basing your strike price decisions on how you think the stock will be performing between now and the time the option that you are considering will expire."

Ernie had a question. "In deciding which option contract to write, did you say we should be looking on the template at the 'Total Annual Yield' column or the 'Annual Yield With Capital Appreciation' column?"

"There is no assurance that your stock will rise to the strike price at expiration, which is reflected in the 'Annual Yield With Capital Appreciation.' Therefore, the most realistic and conservative way to evaluate this would be to look primarily at the 'Total Annual Yield' for your decisions. Then you should balance out all of your decisions to reach your twelve-percent target return. That way you can consider the capital appreciation as 'icing on the cake' if it happens," Max responded.

ONLINE COVERED CALL OPTION TRADING

"So, after considering the alternatives, you've made a decision on a call option to write. At this point you are now ready to use the online brokerage to execute the option transaction. What you need to do now when you are logged on to your brokerage account is to go to the Web page online that is used for option trades.

"Go back to the first worksheet I gave you for your six stocks. Let's assume that you are going to execute the trade in the second row on the printout for BBB Technologies...namely, you are going to write 30 contracts of the October $20 calls. The option symbol is BBBJD and the current quote midpoint is $1.30.

"The information required by different brokers for their online system should be essentially the same. The pieces of it may just be located in different places on their Web pages. You will become familiar with your broker's pages very quickly after you do a few option trades.

"There should appear several choices for the kind of option trade you wish to place. The buyer of an option would click on 'buy' to purchase a call option or 'sell' in order to sell it. As you are not a buyer, but are a writer of call options, to initiate a new transaction you will always click on 'sell-to-open' or 'sell covered call,' however it is termed by your brokerage. You are selling...that is, writing...the option, and the transaction is an opening transaction. You will enter the number of contracts, remembering that one option contract is for one hundred shares of the underlying stock. In this example you would enter 30. You then need to type in the option symbol in the appropriate place to be sure you get the right contract. Get this information from your template.

"There will also be a section that will ask you to click whether you wish a **'market order'** or a **'limit order.'** A limit order requires that a **'limit price'** be set.

"If you select market order, the transaction will be carried out at the 'best price available' when the order reaches the marketplace. It assures that the transaction will be executed at some price. The difficulty with options sometimes is that they are not as liquid as the underlying stock. Here's what I mean. BBB Technologies common stock trades millions of shares per day, but there are not millions of call options for BBB Technologies that trade daily. The number of option contracts traded in a day is much, much smaller. As a result, even though there is a highly efficient, fungible market for options, sometimes the difference between the bid and ask can be wide and can change to an investor's disadvantage if a market order is placed. You could then end up getting your order filled for something less than the price you were expecting. For that reason, I suggest that you *always use limit orders and set a limit price* for your option trades. While you will not be guaranteed that your order will be filled, you will be assured that if it is filled the price you will receive will not be less than the limit price you have set...and it may be more, depending on the best price available at the time.

"So, you should click on 'limit order' and then set a limit price you are willing to accept. Since your transaction will not be completed for less than the limit price, you need to be sure that the amount you set is either at the midpoint between the bid and ask or perhaps even a bit lower to give greater assurance that the transaction will be completed. For example, if the bid on your option transaction is $1.10 and the ask is $1.50, to have a reasonable assurance that your order will get filled, you should bid about $1.30. Or, you could plug $1.20 into your calculation template, and if that amount would result in a return that is acceptable, you could consider entering your limit order for $1.20.

"The risk is that if you enter a market order you will often get filled at the bottom end, namely the bid of $1.10 in this case, or even lower on occasion. By setting a realistic limit order price, you can almost always get your transaction completed and assure yourself that you are getting a reasonable market price for your option trades.

"If you were to put in a limit price that is a bit higher than the midpoint between the bid and ask, it would probably take a rise in the price of the underlying stock and correspondingly the option, before your trade would be executed. Since there would be no assurance that the price would go up, your order might not be filled.

"There is one risk you do run, however, when setting a limit price. If by the time you get your order placed the price of the underlying stock has declined, then the option price will have also declined and your order will not be filled unless the price of the stock and the option rise again. The best guard against this is to be sure you have a very current quote on the bid and ask for the option contract and that you enter your limit order as quickly as possible after you have made your decision to write the option. In the event the price of the stock declines, however, you should be prepared to cancel your option order and replace it with a lower limit price. Otherwise you would need to wait to see if the market recovers to your price.

"Of course, if the bid price fulfills your return objective and is acceptable to you, you could actually enter the bid amount as your price, but you should typically try to do at least somewhat better than that. You can plug in quotes for various premium alternatives into your template to see what the yields look like compared with your objective."

"Is this any different from placing a limit order on a stock?" Ernie asked.

"No, it's the same concept," Max responded. "It may be even more important, however, due to the smaller volumes of option contracts traded. In that regard, there's another element I'd like to mention for you to consider. That's an **'all-or-none order.'**

"When initiating an option trade, 'all or none' is a further restricting element of a limit order whereby you specify that either your entire order be executed at the same time or none of it is to be executed. For example, if you are trying to sell-to-open ten call contracts, it is possible that only part of your order might be filled...say two contracts, with the order for the other eight not filled if the price of the option should quickly back off of your limit price. If you have to go in later and alter your price to fill the rest of your order, or if the balance of your limit order is not filled until a later date, your commission costs would go up. These trades would be treated as separate transactions for commission purposes.

"The 'all or none order' is a good idea, particularly when you are dealing with options that are thinly traded. It's not always possible to know how liquid the market is for the options you are trading. As you gain more experience with option trading you will get a feel for this. You should also be able to get volume information on option contracts from your broker's quotation system. At least initially it may be advisable for you to use 'all or none' orders to avoid partial order fills. "

"How do you specify 'all or none,' Max," Karie inquired.

"When you are initiating your transaction, either online or through an automated voice response phone system, there will be an area on your screen or you will be asked whether you wish to place any special conditions on the transaction. This will give you an opportunity to indicate if you wish the order to be 'all or none.'

"There's one final element I would add. You also have an opportunity to indicate the time-in-force of the transaction. You can specify that the order will only be valid for the day, referred to as a **'day order,'** or that it will be a **'good-'til-canceled order,'** also referred to as **'GTC.'** I don't have any recommendation as to which you should use. That would be entirely up to you. I tend to use orders that are valid only for the day I am placing the order. If the order is not filled, that gives me an opportunity to reevaluate what I want to do at that point and enter a new order for the following day."

"Option trading sounds more complicated to me than what we go through to just buy or sell a stock online," Karie indicated.

"The process is actually pretty much the same, Karie," Max indicated. "Since you are looking up quite a few quotes, computing a midpoint between bid and ask, and entering the information into the template for review, it just seems more complicated. It is more work with options, but the end result definitely justifies it. And the more trades you do, the easier it will get. After doing my template research in advance, I have gotten to the point where I can place a market order for new shares of a stock, place a limit order on covered calls for the stock and have both orders filled, all within about thirty seconds.

"Once you have entered your order, you can check your online account at any time to see if the order is still pending or if it has been executed. Until it is filled, you will probably want to continue to monitor the price of the underlying stock and the option to see if you need to make any adjustment to your limit price if the market declines. Or you may wish to wait it out to see if the market recovers to your price.

"In addition to receiving a brokerage statement periodically in the mail, you can, of course, also check at any time online to see a current statement of positions and cash balances as well as a transaction history. When you have written covered calls, the calls will show up online and on your brokerage statements as a negative balance until the options either expire or are assigned. This is a **"short position"** offset to the cash you received into your account. It will reflect the current market price of the options as they fluctuate up and down based upon the price of the underlying stock. As we've discussed, in addition to the price of the underlying stock, the other variable that will affect the price of the option is the time remaining until expiration. If the price of the stock were to remain constant after the trade, the negative balance of the option on your brokerage statement would gradually diminish to zero as time dwindles to the expiration date."

"Just credit my account with the money tomorrow," Ernie chimed in eagerly. "Retirement...here we come!"

PRACTICAL APPLICATIONS FOR MAKING MONEY

If you do not already have a discount brokerage account, check out several of the online brokerages listed in the "Discount Brokerages" section of the Appendix entitled "Investment Web Sites on the Internet." If you do not use a computer, call the brokerages by phone at the numbers provided to obtain information. Compare them with each other by answering the following questions:

	Broker #1	Broker #2	Broker #3
Name of brokerage			
Stock commissions charged			
Options commissions charged (flat fee component)			
Options commissions charged (per contract fee)			
Interest paid on cash balances			
Availability of human representatives			
Other: _______________			
Other: _______________			
Other: _______________			

If you have already established a brokerage account, it is important that you become familiar with the Web pages and/or the automated voice response phone system that is available for option trading. If you plan to use the automated voice response phone system it would be best to obtain the brokerage's written literature that describes how the system is operated. This would especially be needed for obtaining quotes on options. Other elements of the system may be practiced simply by dialing the brokerages automated voice response phone number and using the touch-tone buttons on your phone to reach the appropriate activity associated with option trades as directed by the recorded voice.

After logging onto your brokerage's Internet Web site and accessing your account, click on the button for trading options and look at all of the Web pages associated with option trading and quotations. Note any questions you have about trading or quotations regarding the brokerage's Web site or the automated voice response phone system. Then call a human representative at your brokerage to get your questions answered.

TRACKING YOUR RESULTS

11

> A billion here, a billion there, and pretty soon you're talking about real money.
>
> Senator Everett Dirkson

"Now that you are ready to start your option writing program," Max said, switching to a new subject, "it's important that you have a mechanism to keep track of how you are doing on an ongoing basis compared with your objective. To accomplish that, I've created another template using Excel. The CD I gave you also has this file on it, which is called 'results.'"

(You, Reader/Investor, have this file on the CD you've used previously. There is also an instruction page in the Appendix outlining exactly what data to enter into the template. Worksheets are included at the end of the book for those who are not using a computer.)

"Here is a sample of how you would use this file template," Max said as he handed them an example sheet.

"The appearance is reminiscent of the 'calls' file, but serves a different purpose. Let's go over it briefly. Again, the 'x' at the top in some of the columns means you need to type in that information. Otherwise the template makes the calculations. There are a few more columns with an 'x' in this template. I think it should all be pretty clear.

SORTED BY TRADE

X	X	X	X		X	X	X	X	X	X	X	X	
				MARKET	TRADE				OPTION		PREM.	STOCK	$	%
ACCT.	STOCK	SHS.	COST	VALUE	DATE	EXPIR.	STRIKE	DAYS	SYMBOL	PREM.	INC.	GAIN/LOSS	RETURN	RETURN
PER	BBB	3,000	$18.00	$54,060	1-Jul-03	19-Oct-03	$20.00	110	BBBJD	$1.35	$4,007	$0	$4,007	24.60%
IRA	KKK	1,000	$48.90	$48,920	5-Jul-03	21-Dec-03	$50.00	169	KKKLJ	$2.95	$2,913	$1,100	$4,013	17.71%
											$6,920	$1,100		

To start you need to enter the account type in the first column. This is particularly handy, as we'll see in a minute, if you have more than one account. I would suggest that you enter 'PER' in this column for transactions having to do with your taxable personal account. Use 'IRA' for your IRA account. You can obviously use whatever designation you wish, as long as you are consistent. If you had only one brokerage account, you could leave this column blank. In the column before the expiration date, you enter the date of the trade. If, for example, the trade date was August 15, 2001, you would type 8/15/2001 into the cell. You also need to enter the net amount of the premium income as shown in your brokerage confirmation. Also, if your stock is called away from you or otherwise sold, you need to determine the gain or loss on the stock (the amount of capital appreciation or capital depreciation realized based upon the price of the stock on the date when the calls were written or based upon your cost basis, whichever is more meaningful for you) and enter that information in total dollars as well. That's all there is to it. In the unusual circumstance that you bought back your call options prior to expiration, you would need to reduce the amount of premium income you received by the amount you paid to buy back the options.

"You can see in the first example that this option writer wrote 30 call contracts of the BBB Technologies October $20 calls in a personal taxable account and received $4,007 in premium income. As the option expired unexercised, there was no sale of the stock and therefore no gain or loss. The annualized percentage return was 24.60%. In the second example, the option writer wrote 10 call contracts in an IRA of the KKK Industries December $50 calls and received $2,913. At expiration the stock was priced above $50, so the stock was called away. The investor's gain on the stock during the period of this trade was $1,100. In this case, the dollar return column shows the combined premium income and gain on the stock of $4,013 for a total annualized percentage return from the premium income and capital appreciation on the stock of 17.71%.

"You will see that at the top left hand corner of the worksheet it says 'Sorted By Trade.' I'm sure you know that Excel has a sorting capability, and we can use that to our advantage with this template. You can see on your computer screen at the bottom left of the worksheet on the template itself that there are four tabs labeled 'Trade Sort,' 'Expiration Sort,' 'Stock Sort' and 'Account Sort.' The 'Trade Sort' template is the one we've been talking about so far, and it should be used as your primary results template for entering data. The others are available for your use if you decide it is important for you to be able to look at your results information sorted by expiration date, or by stock, or by account. Obviously the last one would only apply if you have more than one brokerage account where you are writing options.

"The best time to enter the information into the 'Trade Sort' template is when you get your broker confirmations in the mail and when options expire. Or, you can get the information online after the trade is executed. Here's what to do if you want to use the other sorting methods. Start by going to the 'Trade Sort' template and highlight all of the data by placing the cursor in the upper left hand cell where your data starts. Click on your mouse button while holding it down and drag the cursor to the right and down until it darkens all of the data cells on your worksheet. Then let go of the mouse button and all of your data will be selected. Now click on the 'Copy' icon at the top and then click on the tab at the bottom you wish to use. It will take you to that tab, which has the same appearance as the worksheet you see here. Point and click the cursor into the same cell address as the cell from which you started copying the data. Then all you have to do is click on the 'Paste' icon and all of the data you copied will be pasted into the new worksheet. I've formatted each of the tabbed worksheets so that they will sort according to what the tab says. So all you need to do now is keep the data highlighted and then click on the word 'Data' at the top. A drop down menu box will appear. Click on 'Sort' and another drop down menu comes up. Just click on the 'OK' box at the bottom and your data is sorted.

"It can be useful to look at your data by stock, for example, so that you can see how many times you have written options on a specific stock and how it has worked out for you. That will give you a very good feel for the market over time. You can also enter data into the other tabs and sort by expiration date or by account type."

PRACTICAL APPLICATIONS FOR MAKING MONEY

PRACTICING CALL CONTRACT SELECTION

Select several stocks you either own or that are on your personal "buy list." Using the Excel template "calls" and your brokerage account, complete the data on the template for each stock, selecting several hypothetical covered call option opportunities. Refer to the section entitled "How to Use the Microsoft® Excel Template 'Calls' to Calculate Covered Call Writing Opportunities" in the Appendix for assistance if needed. If you do not have access to the Internet, use your brokerage's automated voice response phone system to obtain the necessary information or call a human representative at the brokerage if needed. Refer to the section entitled "How to Use a Discount Broker Without a Computer and Calculating Covered Call Writing Opportunities Manually" in the Appendix for assistance if needed. It may also be helpful to refer to the section of the Appendix entitled "How to Determine the Symbol for an Option."

Review the results of your calculations and think about which option writing choices you would make if you were trading for real and why you made these selections.

<u>PRACTICING TRACKING YOUR RESULTS</u>

Select several of the option trades you have chosen above and practice entering the data into the Excel template "results." Enter a hypothetical gain or loss on the stocks to observe what effect they have on your dollar return and percent return calculations.

THE TAXMAN COMETH

12

> Dear Internal Revenue Service:
>
> I haven't been able to sleep because of all the income I didn't report on my tax return, so I'm enclosing a cashier's check. If I still can't sleep, I'll send you the rest.
>
> Anonymous

"And now," Max sighed, "I have to give you some boring information of a different kind. Do you remember what I said about Liz Taylor's last wedding night?"

"Yes, Max," Karie sighed back. "No need to remind us. Let's get back to the boring information!"

TAXABLE ACCOUNTS

"Sure," Max concurred. "Actually, there is some good news here to go with the boredom. I'll give you the good, the bad, and the ugly. People always say they wish they had a big tax problem...until they actually have one, that is, and then they wish it was gone. When you have success with a call option writing strategy in a personal account it's going to mean more income taxes to pay. But, on the other hand, you are going to have a lot more income than you otherwise would have had, so that obviously more than makes up for it."

"Well, that's positive. The income will exceed the taxes! Is there any more good news, Max?" Ernie inquired.

"Well, how about this? As we've said earlier, when you write call options you get the premium income up front into your account the next day to use as you wish. The good news from a tax standpoint is that *even though you have the use of the premium income immediately, it isn't taxed to you until the options expire* or until you close out your position if you buy-to-close, whichever occurs first. That can lead to some tax planning opportunities at times, depending on the time of year and the expiration date on the options you are writing."

"Sounds like terrific news. How does that work?" Karie asked.

"Let's say that you wrote options on your KKK stock with a July expiration date and the options expired without your stock being called away. Now you are ready to write another option. You look at the premiums that are available for various expiration dates. You also look at your tax picture and realize that you have built up a lot of taxable income during this tax year and you would like to try to defer some taxable income into the next tax year. What you could do is to select one of the call options with an expiration in January or later of next year. That way the premium income you receive on those options now will not be taxed to you until the options expire, which would be in the next tax year. You have just deferred the income tax consequence into next year, even though you have the money right now. And you can do this with as many different stocks and options contracts as you like. This can give you a pretty powerful tax planning tool at times.

"Speaking of tax consequences, perhaps the most important point is that the premium income you receive from writing calls is **'capital gain'** for tax purposes. The bad news is that the premiums are almost always **'short-term'** capital gain regardless of the length of time the call was outstanding. That means your option writing income is usually taxed at the same rate as if it were **'ordinary income.'** You will need to report your option trades on Schedule D of Form 1040.

"And, if you would decide to close out your option position by buying back the options, any gain or loss would be short-term capital gain or loss in the year that the position was closed out. For example, let's say you wrote options in July that were not due to expire until the following year and you received $3,000 in premium income. In November you bought back the options for $1,000. You would have a short-term capital gain of $2,000 for the tax year in which you bought back the options, not in the next tax year when the options would have otherwise expired."

CAPITAL GAIN VS. CAPITAL APPRECIATION

Karie looked puzzled. "Max, you've used the term 'capital appreciation' frequently in our discussions, and now you refer to 'capital gain.' I'm not sure I understand the difference."

"There is an important difference, Karie," Max responded. "When we are talking about capital appreciation, it is an investment term that simply means an increase in value of a security, such as a stock or an option. For example, if a stock goes from $35 to $50, it has experienced capital appreciation of $15 per share. Capital gain is a tax term that comes into play only when a capital asset, such as a stock or option, is liquidated. It occurs when the proceeds from the sale of a stock or an option is greater than its cost."

"I follow you. Thanks, Max."

"I'm sure you are aware that if you have capital gains you can offset them with capital losses to reduce your tax burden," Max continued. "So, if you had some stock you took a loss on, you could use that loss to offset some of the gains you realize on your option writing income."

"That would help," Ernie indicated. "Actually, Max, we have a **'capital loss'** on some stocks carried forward from the previous tax year. If we had some gains from writing call options, could we use those prior losses to offset the gains on the option income?"

"Yes, you can," Max responded. "That would be an excellent use of any losses you have incurred in the past. Or for any current **'unrealized loss'** in any of your stocks, you could sell those stocks and use the realized capital losses to offset option writing income."

"That works for me!" Ernie said.

Max continued. "The tax effect on stock you have owned for a long time may be different, and beneficial to you, if your calls are assigned and your stock is sold to the option holder at expiration. If you sell calls and the calls are assigned, the strike price at which you sell your stock *plus* the premium you received becomes the sale price of the stock to determine the amount of gain or loss. Let's say you had paid $20 per share several years ago for your stock. The stock was trading at $42, and you had written call options on it for a premium of $2 per share at a strike price of $45. On expiration the stock was called away from you at the strike price. Your gain would be $45 minus $20 plus $2, or $27 per share. When your stock is assigned, the resulting gain or loss depends upon the cost of the underlying stock delivered and the holding period of the stock. What I mean by 'holding period' is the length of time you have owned the stock. In this case, because you had held the stock for a long enough time period to have it qualify for **'long-term'** capital gain treatment, the gain on your stock *and the option premium* will be long-term capital gain at a favorable tax rate! So, this is the exception when an option premium is taxed as a long-term capital gain rather than a short-term capital gain.

"Here's the rule. Writing an at-the-money or an out-of-the-money covered call does not affect the holding period of the underlying stock for purposes of determining whether any gain is long-term or short-term if the stock is eventually assigned. This will cover almost all of the transactions you will be doing. As I've said before, I almost never recommend writing in-the-money call options. The tax consequences on in-the-money transactions can sometimes become more complicated too, especially if the underlying stock would qualify as a long-term holding for tax purposes. I doubt that you would be doing any such transaction, but you should consult your tax advisor if you did. And there's always talk about possible changes in the tax rates for capital gains based on the holding period, so it's a good idea to keep up with that or to consult your tax advisor.

"Oh, one last thing," Max said. "We talked about buying stocks on margin and writing options on them. If you did that, and if you itemize deductions on your tax returns, you should be able to take the investment interest expense as an itemized deduction up to the combined amount of any interest income and dividend income you report on your tax return. Remember, the premium income from option writing is capital gain, not interest income. If your investment interest expense exceeds your combined interest and dividend income, then the excess interest expense can be carried over as a deduction to the following tax year.

"It's always a good idea to consult your tax advisor about all of these tax matters we have discussed. As you know, the laws are cumbersome and they can always change…so, as my high school principal always said, 'A word to the wise is sufficient!' I never really understood what he meant by that, but he always sounded so intelligent when he said it!"

"Seems like you have to be a statistician to keep track of all this," Ernie commented.

"Well," Max responded, "it is a bit more work, but well worth the effort when you consider what you have to gain. You will easily get used to it. A statistician is nothing more than someone who is good with numbers but lacks the personality to be an accountant. That certainly doesn't describe you, Ernie!"

Karie had trouble deciding whether to groan or laugh.

"Max," Ernie, deep in thought, chimed in, "I've had something in the back of my mind for awhile, and this seems to be the best time to ask you about it. We've got a couple of stocks we've owned for a long time that are now worth many times what we paid for them. They would be just as good for call option writing as the other stocks we own, but there is one thing that worries me."

"I think I know where you are headed with this, Ernie," Max countered. "What's your concern?"

"Well, I know you said that the downside to writing calls on stocks is when the price of the stock goes well beyond the strike price plus the premium income per share at expiration. Then the stock is called away from you at less overall gain than if you had just held onto the stock alone. I know that you've still made money on this transaction, because you've collected the premium income and you've gotten the additional capital appreciation as the stock went up in value from its price on the day the option was written to the strike price. So, I can see that there is an upside to the downside from that perspective."

Max and Karie listened closely.

"But there would seem to me to be an additional downside if these stocks were called away from us. We would have a sizeable capital gain and would have to pay taxes on it, right?"

Karie smiled and nodded her head, acknowledging the potential wrinkle that Ernie had uncovered.

"I thought that was it, Ernie. You have made a very important point that we need to discuss, and there are some solutions," Max said reassuringly.

THE CHALLENGE OF WRITING CALLS
ON HIGHLY APPRECIATED STOCK

"As Ben Franklin said a few years back, there are only two certainties in life...death and taxes. I suppose that we all generally accept this, but we'd like to be able to plan for both of them. As far as capital gains tax is concerned, we are used to having the certainty of timing it so that our best tax interests are served. When we are writing covered calls on stocks we own that have grown in value substantially, we never know exactly when that big capital gain might be triggered through an exercise of the option causing a sale of the stock.

"First, you should never write a call option on a stock that you are absolutely unwilling to sell. But the opportunity to earn call option premium income may outweigh the possibility that the stock might be called away, triggering an unwanted capital gain. One choice might be to write calls on only a portion of the stock. If it is called away, you would only have a portion of the total gain taxed to you."

"That way if the stock price went up you could write options on the rest of the stock at a higher strike price and structure it so the expiration date falls into the next tax year to spread out the potential tax on the gains if the rest of the stock is called away," Ernie responded.

"Correct," Max concurred. "Also, keep in mind that there are favorable tax laws for long-term capital gains on the sale of stock. Under current law, for taxpayers in higher brackets, you would pay a lot less on the capital gain than you would on your ordinary income. I know that's not much consolation if you are facing taxes on a big gain, but unless you donate the stock to a charity or die owning it, taxes on the gain will be paid by someone at some point. Also Congress has been known to change the tax laws with some regularity. While we would hope any changes would be in our favor, there's no assurance that the tax on capital gains won't be greater at some point in the future than it is today."

"I understand what you are saying, Max," Ernie said, "but if you really don't want to trigger the capital gain, and you really do want to write options on the stock, is there anything you can do?"

"You're a great straight man, Ernie!" Max chuckled. "I do have a suggestion for how to deal with this.

"Let's assume that you have written calls on a stock with a large unrealized long-term capital gain and that the price of this stock has gone up above the strike price of the calls you have written. As we discussed before, options are usually not exercised until expiration, even though the buyer of the option has the right to exercise them at any time up through the expiration date. So, if you are, say, well within a month of expiration, and the price of the stock is above the strike price of the calls, here is what you may wish to consider doing. This is a case where it may be advantageous to act before the expiration date. You can buy back the call contracts at the current market price to close out your option position, and then write new calls with a different and more distant expiration date.

"This, in effect, would dispose of the old call option and defer the exercise of the new call option until a later date. If the new options have the same strike price as the old ones, the option premium on the new calls will always be greater than your cost in buying back the old calls. You could, of course, have a gain or loss on the old options when you buy them back. It would largely depend on how much the market value of the stock went above the strike price of the original calls...in other words, how much intrinsic value there is.

"There is a name for this. Buying back your calls and then writing new calls at the same strike price, but with a more distant expiration is called 'rolling forward.'"

Karie was fidgeting in her chair, which meant that further explanation was needed. "Max, what language was it that you were just speaking?" she inquired facetiously.

That brought a laugh from both Max and Ernie.

"I'll try to translate it into English, Karie. The best way to do that is the way we've done it before...with an example." Max leaned back in his high-back swivel chair, rocking slightly and looking briefly at the ceiling for guidance as he collected his thoughts.

"Let's say you bought shares of AAA stock ten years ago. You now own 1,000 shares and your cost basis, adjusted for several stock splits, is only $5 per share. About 2 ½ months ago the market value of the stock was $50 per share, or $50,000 worth of the stock. At that time you sold ten call contracts on your AAA shares at a strike price of $55. Since then two months have passed and the options expire about two weeks from now.

"When you wrote the options you collected a premium of $2.50 per share for total premium income of $2,500. From the date you wrote the options 2 ½ months ago the price of the stock has gone from $50 to its current price of $57 per share. The call contracts you wrote are now priced at $3.50 reflecting the current intrinsic value of $2 per share (the $57 current market value less the $55 strike price) and the remaining time value of $1.50 per share (the $3.50 current market less the $2 intrinsic value). If you hold your position where it is now, and the price of the stock remains above $55, you will realize a capital gain of $50 per share (the $55 strike price less your $5 cost basis) or $50,000 when the stock is called away from you.

"Not wanting to pay the capital gains taxes at this time, you decide that rolling forward is a strategy that makes sense for you. You get quotes from your broker on calls with the same strike price, but with a longer expiration date. There are several option expiration dates available to you. Which one you select is purely a matter of preference and planning. You might want to take into consideration the expiration dates of calls currently existing that you have written on other stocks for purposes of expiration diversification. After review, you decide on the contract at the same strike price and with an expiration date in about 6½ months. If your stock were called away at this new expiration date, it would place the capital gain into the next tax year, which would be more acceptable to you. Of course, it's always possible that the stock price may decline below the $55 strike price by the new expiration date, in which case you would keep your stock and the new option premium income. There would be no capital gain realized on the stock and therefore no taxes to pay in that event…just tax to pay on the short-term capital gain from the premium income.

"The price of the option contract with the new expiration date is $5.50 (larger due to the longer expiration term). You are ready to roll forward.

"First you buy back the old option contracts at $3.50 with an order to buy to close ten contracts. After the order is filled, you then sell-to-open (also termed 'sell covered call') ten contracts of the new option at $5.50. When that order is filled, you watch what happens until the new option expiration date approaches."

"So, we've been talking all about taxes, Max," Karie interjected. "What's the tax result of all of these machinations?"

"It sounds a lot more complicated than it really is, Karie," Max continued. "Let's first consider the sale and repurchase of the first option. You sold the initial calls for $2,500 and repurchased them for $3,500 for a loss of $1,000. This loss can be used to offset other capital gains you've earned. The new option transaction stands on its own. If held until expiration, the premium income of $5,500 would be taxed the same as other option transactions we've previously discussed. Of course, if the stock is called away at the new option's expiration you would still have a $50,000 long-term capital gain to pay tax on."

"So, what have you really accomplished by doing this?" Karie inquired.

"You've bought additional time and thereby have extended out the realization of the capital gain and the corresponding tax on it. And, as we've said, if the stock were to go down again below the strike price at expiration, the capital gain tax would be a moot issue."

"But what if the stock just continues to go up and up?" Karie wanted to know.

"Good question, Karie," Max acknowledged. "There are a couple of choices you would have. First, you could just continue to roll forward the expiration dates by buying back the older contracts and writing new options as each expiration date approaches, just as we did in this example. The higher the price rises, however, the more likely it becomes that your stock will eventually be called away from you at the $55 strike price at some point. So, if your stock keeps rising, this strategy is simply one of deferral of the capital gain recognition to a time when it may be more acceptable from a tax planning standpoint than the present.

"Going back to the example, another alternative would be to buy back the first call options and then write new calls with a higher strike price. This is referred to as 'rolling up.' Doing this can take the pressure off a bit, because if the strike price on the new option was $60, for example, you now have out-of-the-money calls that wouldn't be exercised at expiration unless the stock continued to rise. If it did go up further, your stock would be called away at $60, not $55, and you would have a $55,000 capital gain subject to tax."

"That sounds like a pretty attractive alternative, even with the tax to be paid," Ernie offered. "Wouldn't that be the best strategy?"

"It could be," Max responded. "But, of course, the premium you would receive on a call with a $60 strike price would be quite a bit less than one with a $55 strike price. As you know from our previous discussion, the higher the strike price for a call option, the lower the premium. Depending on how much higher the strike price is on the new option compared to the old option, and also how much further out the expiration is extended, the premium income on the new calls could be significantly reduced. You would have to consider all of the options, no pun intended. The best choice in some cases might be a combination of rolling forward and rolling up. A lot depends on what is going to happen later. Unfortunately, of course, we can't predict the future.

"There's one additional alternative you should know about. It's not likely that you would use it often, if ever. But in a situation like this you might consider it. When you write calls on your stock and your stock is assigned, that doesn't mean that you have to deliver exactly those same shares. Like option contracts, shares of stock are fungible. That is to say, shares are freely interchangeable among investors. The buyer of your stock subject to the calls doesn't care whether you deliver the shares you owned at the time your calls were written or different shares. Their fungibility makes them all the same. Therefore, if you would prefer not to deliver the shares you own, you can always purchase new shares on the open market and deliver them to fulfill your assignment obligation in place of the original shares you own. This would create an immediate capital loss rather than triggering the capital gain that would be realized by selling your original shares (as the market price you pay for these new shares would be higher than the strike price you are paid for the shares), but that might also work to your advantage. You would, of course, need available cash or margin borrowing capability to buy these new shares to do this.

"You can see why it is always best to write options on stocks that you don't mind being called away from you at expiration. You just let the stock be called away and accept your gains rather than having to chase a rising stock by rolling forward and/or rolling up. Nonetheless, these are workable ways to handle the writing of call options on highly appreciated stock when the price of the stock rises. It's best to have a plan at the very start so that if the stock price increases significantly you know pretty well in advance what action you will want to take. As we've said, about eighty-percent of options that are out-of-the-money when written expire unexercised, so this scenario is not something you would frequently have to face...but forewarned is forearmed!"

Max's assistant brought in a badly needed pot of coffee, as all three were obviously ready for a respite.

TAX DEFERRED ACCOUNTS

"And now," Max added, "I've saved the best news for last. None of this tax stuff applies when you are dealing with a tax-deferred account, such as an IRA, since no income or gain is taxed until actual distributions are made from the account. That gives an investor a tremendous opportunity to earn a large amount of current premium income and not pay any taxes on it until withdrawals are made from the account. End of story!"

"Whew," Ernie sighed, "I'm glad that's over!" Karie pretended to wipe her brow with the back of her hand and nodded in full concurrence.

"Before you get too comfortable," Max continued, "I have to let you know that there is one more subject we need to cover at our last session next week."

"So, this was just the end of the chapter and not the end of the story, huh?" Ernie chided.

"Well, you do want to be enlightened with the whole story, don't you?" Max inquired. "Can you handle one more week?"

"Partial enlightenment wouldn't do at all, Max. We want the whole enchilada!" Karie responded. "Is it a more exciting subject than taxes I hope, or do we have to hear more about Liz Taylor's last wedding night?"

"I'll let you make that determination. We need to talk about the important subject of how the markets are affected by economics and whether you should always be in the market or whether you should try to time your investment decisions based on what is going on in the economy."

"Economics...the dismal science," Karie groaned. "Are we good for one more week, Ernie?" she asked jokingly.

"We wouldn't want the loss of any of The Guru's details to cut us out of our twelve-percent return now, would we?" Ernie quipped back.

"Good then," Max responded with a firm slap on his knee. "See you next Friday for Econ 101 ½."

"Econ 101 ½?" Ernie asked quizzically.

"Sure," Max countered. "When we're talking about economic projections, about half of the economists believe one thing and the other half believe something else. The trick is to, first, understand what they are saying and then to decide if either half is right!"

PRACTICAL APPLICATIONS FOR MAKING MONEY

This would be a good time to assess whether you have any "realized" capital gains or losses (gains or losses resulting from actual trades completed) in the current tax year or a carryover from previous tax years that can be used to offset gains or losses on options transactions. Your covered call options writing trades will almost always result in capital gain. Research your records, if applicable, and list any capital gains or losses that would offset future capital gains or losses from your call option trades. Also, give consideration to unrealized losses that could be used if desired.

Name of Stock:
Date of Purchase:
Date of Sale:
Purchase Price:
Sale Price:
Gain:
Loss:

Gain (Loss) Reconciliation:

(a) Tax loss carry forward (if any) from
   prior tax years

(b) Total realized gains in this tax year
   from above

(c) Total realized losses in this tax year
   from above

(d) Net gain (loss) in this tax year – subtract
(c) from (b)   __________

(e) Net gain (loss) to offset option writing gain (loss) –
combine (d) and (a)

TIME IN THE MARKET VS. TIMING THE MARKET

October...this is one of the peculiarly dangerous months to speculate in stocks. The others are July, September, April, November, May, March, January, June, December, August, and February.

Mark Twain

The final Friday arrived quickly. Ernie and Karie soon found themselves back in Max's office, anxious to finish their final session and to start using their new investment knowledge.

As usual, Max greeted them warmly and began his tutorial. "There's a general belief in the investment industry that 'time in the market' is what counts, not 'timing the market.' This is what we'll talk about today in our final session."

Karie looked puzzled. "I thought we were going to talk about economics, Max," she said. "And what does that mean...time in the market and timing the market?"

"It raises the question of whether you should be invested in the stock market all of the time, or whether there are periods of time that you should be out of the market, depending on what is going on in the world," Max responded. "And, yes, we are going to talk about economics, because economic events, or at least the perception of them, is one determinant for what happens to the stock market.

WHEN TO BE IN THE MARKET

"First," Max emphasized by raising his index finger into the air, "I strongly believe that almost no one has the ability to consistently and accurately predict what will happen in the future with the economy. This includes individual investors, institutional investors, and the economists themselves.

"This implies, then, that investors in stocks should probably be in the market all of the time and not try to guess when it's a good time to get in and out based on their perceptions of what is happening in the economy. There are some months that tend to be better than others for the market, but it's certainly not always or even often predictable."

Karie was curious. "Are there some times of the year that seem to be worse for the market than others, Max?" she asked.

"September and October traditionally are thought to be the worst months…however not always. In the past decade or so, August has often proven to be difficult. But even though I believe we should probably be in the market all the time, I think it's a very good idea to keep some fundamental principles in mind about economics to help guide our decisions. There may come a time when an understanding about economics can give us a strong feeling about what action we should take. Rather than trying to second guess whether we should be in or out of the market though, what I'm suggesting to you is that a good knowledge of these economic fundamentals can help you make quality decisions about how to structure your call option writing program."

"Oh, good!" Ernie jumped in. "I was afraid this wasn't going to relate directly to option writing. If focusing in on some ideas about economics can help us make more informed option writing decisions, then so much the better."

"It may help," Max responded. "A little knowledge can be a dangerous thing, as everyone knows, so this will just be information to keep tucked into the back of your minds so that if the economic winds begin to shift it can perhaps help you see what's coming."

"I think our overriding principle should be that we are in the market at all times unless there is a very compelling reason not to be," Max opined. "Many years ago one wise sage noted that *'the stock market has predicted nine out of the last five recessions!'"*

"That's a rather imperfect record, to say the least!" Ernie chimed in.

"True. But the ups and downs of economic cycles definitely have their effect on the stock market," Max continued. "The problem is that *markets typically go down before a decline in economic activity and head back up before or at the beginning of an economic recovery.* To time investment decisions by predicting economic and business cycles is an art rather than a science. It is a skill almost no one has, including the economists. And that, no doubt, is why it's called the dismal science!

"After all, an economist is simply an expert who will know tomorrow why the things he predicted yesterday didn't happen today!"

"If the smartest economists in the world can't figure it out, Max, why do I need to know about it?" Karie logically inquired.

BEING ALERT FOR ECONOMIC TRENDS

"I think that the ability to identify significant trends as they are happening can perhaps give us a bit of an edge to improve our overall investment returns," Max responded. "Not that we are able to anticipate something before it actually happens. But the ability to see and understand what is happening in the economy can possibly make us more comfortable or uncomfortable with where we are likely headed and may allow us to anticipate a little bit of the future, which in turn can either make or save us money. No guarantees, of course. But knowledge of business cycles and economic trends could help us make a more informed decision, for example, about whether to write a longer-term call versus a shorter-term call; or perhaps whether to write a call with a strike price that is closer to the market price of the stock or more out-of-the-money; or it might even suggest to us that we not write options on some stocks for awhile if we have a strong belief that a very significant market rally may be about to occur."

"Isn't there a risk in doing that, though?" Ernie inquired.

"There is a price to be paid if you are wrong," Max admitted. "Let's say, for example, you think the market will be strong, so you stop writing calls for awhile. If the market stays in a narrow trading range instead, you have missed an opportunity to earn call premium income as a result of your inaction. Or, if the market goes down, you have missed an opportunity to protect yourself on the downside. But, even though economists and knowledgeable investors have a dismal record of predicting the bottom and top turning points in economic cycles, the ability to have some insight early into these cycles can hopefully allow us to save money or make more money than would have otherwise been the case."

"Sounds like it's worth a little time," Ernie acknowledged.

"And that's about all we will give it," Max assured.

THE CONTRARIAN POINT OF VIEW

"One of the themes that has developed over the years is the understanding that securities analysts are often wrong in their assessment of which stocks to buy and at what time. In fact, many investors believe that a contrarian point of view is an appropriate course of action, depending on the analyst's track record. This may also be true of economists and the course of economic activity. When times are exceedingly good and optimism is high, this may be the worst time to be making major new commitments in the stock market. Correspondingly, when pessimism is at its worst it may mean an economic recession has bottomed and the clouds are ready to begin to part. The thought here is not to get too carried away by the prevailing wisdom of 'experts.' The investment world is full of lemmings, and there is no need to jump like Wiley Coyote for the sky and find the edge of a cliff behind you. That's why we are going to talk about some economic fundamentals now.

"Above all, remember that changes in the stock market tend to take place *in advance* of changes in economic activity. When investors correctly or incorrectly perceive harmful or positive effects caused by changes in interest rates, inflation rates and economic decline or growth, the markets as a whole seem to anticipate these events, which generates buying or selling of stocks and other investments.

"Let's get directly to the most important information you need. For starters, we must talk about the Federal Reserve and how they impact interest rates and the supply of money."

Karie yawned and Ernie, the banker, fidgeted.

"This won't be like taking medicine, I promise!" Max laughed. "It will be short and to the point and could make a difference in your investment returns at times, so listen up."

Both of them dutifully straightened themselves in their seats.

Max began. "Alan Greenspan, the long-time chairman of the Federal Reserve, has been a man in the news a lot over the years. The Federal Reserve, called 'the Fed,' is able to have a direct impact on economic activity by affecting interest rates and the supply of money. We won't go into detail on this, but just know that when the Federal Reserve changes short-term interest rates or the supply of money, either up or down, it is trying to control inflation or to invigorate economic growth or employment. For example, between January 2001 and December 2001 the Federal Reserve lowered short-term rates by 475 basis points, or 4 ¾%, an unprecedented amount in such a short time. This strong action was taken to induce positive results in the economy. An understanding of what led to this action and the intended result of it helps us to make more informed investment decisions.

"From a stock investors point of view, changes in interest rates and the growth of the money supply are related to economic growth, and economic growth is related to the price of stocks. The Fed's concern is that such changes be managed properly, because too rapid a decline in interest rates or too great an increase in the money supply can eventually contribute to higher inflation. Typically inflation eventually brings about higher interest rates and a declining stock market. It all sounds pretty simple, but the problem is that the market tends to anticipate changes in interest rates and monetary policy. That means by the time you know about these changes, they have likely already been factored into the market. So, rather than trying to anticipate these events before they happen, which is nearly impossible, our goal should be to try to see major economic trends coming. We can then make more informed investment decisions than if we simply ignored what is happening in the economy.

"What I'd like to do is present several economic scenarios in different stages of a business cycle and discuss how the Fed is likely to act and what it means for investors."

"Keep it simple, Max," Karie pleaded.

"Will do. Here we go."

PEAK IN INFLATION AND INTEREST RATES

"Coming into this stage interest rates and inflation have been increasing for a while and now appear to be approaching the top. The primary way of recognizing this stage is the **'inverted yield curve,'** also known as the 'negative yield curve.' This can be observed very simply by watching the data in financial periodicals or the financial section of most newspapers, on the Internet, or on CNBC's TV network. An inverted yield curve is created when short-term interest rates, for example the three-month Treasury bill, are higher than yields on longer-term bonds such as the ten-year or thirty-year Treasury bond. An inverted yield curve typically occurs when the Fed has been tightening short-term rates to control inflation and the job has been completed. An inverted yield curve is viewed as a condition in which interest rates are now likely to fall.

"As inflation begins to slow down, the Fed increases the money supply and reduces short-term interest rates. It is usually followed by a flattening of the curve, where short-term rates and long-term yields are about equal, and ultimately by a yield curve that turns positive where long-term yields are in their more normal condition of being higher than short-term rates. In this economic situation, financial assets, including stocks, tend to do particularly well, as lower interest rates and reduced inflation are healthy for common stocks. Stocks that are especially sensitive to interest rates, like utilities, commercial banks and consumer cyclicals, such as automobiles, housing, appliances, retailers, leisure, airlines and restaurants should be relatively strong compared to the entire market.

"From an option writing perspective, an investor may wish to write calls that are a bit further out-of-the-money on stocks in these categories, as this will still provide some premium income, but also allow for greater capital appreciation potential in the stocks before they reach their strike prices.

FALLING INFLATION AND INTEREST RATES

"At this stage the yield curve is positive. Inflation and interest rates will continue to fall and eventually remain stable as the Fed stops tinkering with interest rates and the money supply. Unemployment is also falling, capital expenditures by businesses are expanding and the rate by which factories are utilizing their capacity is going up. All of this data can also be monitored in newspapers, on the Internet, and on CNBC. Even though interest rates are no longer declining, stocks should continue to do well as the economy expands and corporate earnings grow. Cyclicals such as steel, machinery and metal are candidates for purchase early in this stage as a strengthening economy increases demand for these companies' products.

"Normal option writing should be done during this stage of the cycle.

INCREASING INFLATION AND INTEREST RATES

"At some point inflation and interest rates begin to increase as the economy continues to grow stronger. Even though corporate profits are high, employee productivity typically begins to decline. The Fed starts to tighten the money supply and interest rates start to increase. This is not the best of times for most stocks, although those with very strong earnings increases can continue to do well. Natural resources stocks, such as those with oil, gas, timber and minerals and also real estate investment trusts tend to do well in this environment.

"As the markets anticipate economic events, this stage implies that stocks may likely start to decline prior to the very peak in economic activity. If an investor ever has a reason to get out of any stocks, this would be the stage to do it. If stocks are held, they should be financially strong companies with low price/earnings ratios and low debt. A market decline or bear market may develop during this stage. So-called 'defensive' stocks seem to perform well relative to other stocks during this stage, as their products are still in demand even during a downturn in the economy. They would include industries such as tobacco, beverage, food, drug and other health care stocks.

"Option writers may wish to write options with a strike price closer to the market price on non-defensive stocks to provide larger premiums and thus greater downside protection. It is less likely that stocks will reach strike prices and be called away in this environment.

SLOWING ECONOMY

"In this stage high interest rates and inflation cause the economy to slow down. Consumer paychecks do not stretch as far as before, and people may not be as willing to use their cash or borrow for costly items such as housing and automobiles. Unemployment is rising. As this stage matures, investors may wish to start accumulating shares in anticipation of the Fed ultimately taking action to reduce interest rates and inflation. Normal option writing should continue during this stage, with strike prices selected either nearer or further from the market price of a given stock depending on how you feel about its short-term prospects and the research provided by your investment advisory services.

"These are the stages of an economic business cycle and some suggestions on what an investor should look for and actions to consider taking. Although I've said that we should generally be in the market all the time, properly assessing where the economy is in its cycle and the direction in which it is headed can help avoid some pitfalls and help increase income and gains or help reduce losses. This is much easier said than done, and, as we've said, economists themselves frequently disagree among themselves. That being the case, be careful not to give too much credence to the analysts' comments about particular stocks and industries without applying what you know yourself and can find out through independent research on the Internet and elsewhere. The 'Timely Buys' recommendations on Zacks will take economic considerations into account, as the recommendations are predicated upon the earnings outlook for individual stocks.

"Of course, these economic scenarios don't always work just as we expect. The bursting of the bubble caused by 'dot com' mania and the excessive capital spending on telecommunications and other equipment caused the economy and markets to react differently than we might have expected. At least it was far more difficult than usual to anticipate. The difficult international tensions have had a destabilizing impact on the markets as well.

"Again, it's important to remember that upward or downward adjustments in stock prices typically come before changes in economic activity. If trends can be picked up early in their cycle, appropriate stock and option strategies can be implemented that hopefully improve our investment results. Sometimes it's best to be a contrarian and not follow the herd instinct.

"Questions?" asked Max.

"I've got one," Ernie announced. "You've said you normally recommend being in the market all the time. With the different kinds of stocks that seem to work best in each stage of the economic cycle, how should a person decide which specific stocks to own...especially when it's so difficult to anticipate the stages of the economic cycle?"

"Excellent question, Ernie," Max responded. "Since even the experts have great difficulty anticipating stages of the economic cycle, it's almost impossible to be switching in and out of stock industry sectors as the stages evolve. That's why we recommend that you have a well-balanced portfolio. You may wish to own some stocks that are appropriate for each stage of the cycle, regardless of where the economy is. This would be another kind of diversification. You should, of course, also always consider the degree of risk you are taking with each individual stock you select. With a balanced portfolio you can then concentrate on what your option writing strategies should be as you perceive changes in the economic cycle. In lieu of a balanced portfolio of individual stocks, an investor can buy Exchange Traded Funds and write options on them to achieve diversification and balance. How does that sound?"

"Makes good sense," Ernie acknowledged.

USING SHORT-TERM INDICATORS TO ASSIST WITH STOCK AND CALL OPTION DECISIONS

"Now..." Max continued, "having said all of this, I'd like to conclude with one more subject about timing that may or may not be of interest to you. We've talked about the longer-term big picture and my own personal conclusion that it's probably best to be in the market most or all of the time. I'd like to consider the subject of the very short term. There are investors who use what is called **'technical analysis'** either in place of, or in addition to **'fundamental analysis'** to assist them in making decisions regarding when to buy or sell stocks and also when to write call options. "

"Oh, oh, Ernie. Here come more terms to learn!" Karie interjected.

"Don't worry. These are not critical to the covered call writing process, but their use may be of some value if you can make them work for you. I'd just like to offer them up for consideration, and you can decide for yourselves if they make any sense for you.

"First, when I refer to fundamental analysis, I'm referring to a decision making process for stock selection or retention that is based on such factors as a company's earnings, examination of financial statements and the quality of its management. In fact, the discussion we just had about taking economic events into consideration is part of the fundamental analysis process.

"On the other hand, technical analysis has to do with the interrelationships between a group of elements relating to a company's securities, such as price level, price movement, volume of trading, and perhaps other factors. Essentially they deal only with perceived demand and supply issues relating to a company's securities. Some investors use them exclusively in their decision making. Others use the 'technical indicators' associated with this analysis along with the fundamental analysis."

"So, what camp do you live in on this, Max?" Ernie asked.

"I believe that a fundamentalist approach should be the foundation for all decisions about investments. But I use some of the technical indicators for two things: (1) to see if they are in agreement with or at odds with fundamental analysis, and (2) to help me decide on the timing to write calls on the stocks I own."

"What do you mean by that second point?" Karie questioned. "Aren't you writing calls on your stocks all the time?"

"Karie, on occasion some of the technical indicators might be saying that there is a likelihood of a short-term positive move in a particular stock or the market in general. Naturally, if I had cash available to buy stock, I'd like to buy it before a rise in the market takes place. Also, if I already owned stock but hadn't written calls on it, or if I had calls that were expiring soon, I'd like to be able to wait until after a rise in the stock has taken place before I write my calls. That way I'd be able to realize more capital appreciation by writing at a higher strike price and perhaps also be able to get more premium income. It would also be less likely that my stock would be called away from me than if I had written my calls before the rise at a lower strike price. There are some other ways that active traders in stocks or options might use technical indicators to initiate action, but these are examples of how I use them on occasion."

"OK, Max," Ernie said. "Better go ahead and fill us in. Will we be able to understand this?"

"It would be beyond our purpose to get too deeply into this subject, Ernie, so what I'd like to do is tell you about a few of these short-term technical indicators and how they work. You can decide then whether they might be meaningful for you and if you want to pursue them further. To follow any of them would require additional work, such as charting, for individual stocks or market indexes. It's important to remember, however, that this is not an exact science. Just because technical indicators would seem to predict an event is no assurance whatsoever that the event will occur. Historical results would indicate that there is some value in this. And, human nature being what it is, if investors believe that these indicators are predictive--and many of them do--then it can become a self-fulfilling prophecy at times."

SUPPORT AND RESISTANCE LEVELS

"'Support' and 'resistance' deal with the supply and demand for stock. Too much available supply means more stock than investors want to purchase, so the stock price goes down. The opposite is true of demand. Demand for more shares of a stock than is available means upward pressure on the price of the stock. If the available supply and the current demand for shares of a stock are equal, then the price pretty much moves sideways.

"Support has to do with a declining stock price, and a chart is necessary to determine support area prices. If a chart for a given stock shows that the price has declined to a certain level more than once--preferably several times--in the past where the decline halted and reversed, this would be considered a support area for the stock. In other words, the supply of stock dried up relative to the demand for it. If the price has been above this support area and it declined down to it again, we might expect that this support area would hold and that the price would either remain at about that level for awhile or head up. So, if we were looking at buying this stock, we might be more attracted to buying it when it reached a support area. If in the past the price had held several times at this level and then reversed upward significantly, we might be inclined to wait until such a rise had occurred again before writing calls. None of this is to say that the price can't just keep going downward. If it does, it simply means that the sellers won the battle over the buyers for the stock, and a new support level would have to be looked for in the chart.

"Resistance, on the other hand, has to do with a rising stock price. Again, a chart is necessary. If a chart for a given stock shows that the price has risen to a certain level more than once--preferably several times--in the past where the rise halted and reversed, this would be considered a resistance area for the stock. Here the supply of stock increased in relationship to the demand. If the price has been below this support area and it rose up to it again, we might expect that this resistance area would hold and that the price would either remain at that level for awhile or head down. So, if we were looking at selling this stock, we might be more attracted to selling it when it reached a resistance area. If in the past the price had held several times at this level and then reversed downward significantly, we might be inclined to either sell the stock or write covered calls that would give us significant premiums for downside protection. Of course, the price could just keep going upward. If it does, it simply means that the buyers won the battle over the sellers for the stock, and a new resistance level would have to be looked for in the chart.

"We often see stocks trade within a price range, with both support and resistance levels being established. When the price eventually breaks out of that range, either on the upside or the downside, it may give us a signal as to which direction the stock will trend at that point."

"Do you have to make these charts yourself, Max?" Karie asked.

"That's one way of doing it, Karie, but obviously this can take quite a bit of time, especially if you are tracking a lot of stocks or market indexes. Fortunately most online brokerages allow you to build custom charts of securities and to add many of these technical indicators to the charts. There is no additional charge for this service. StockCharts.com (www.stockcharts.com) also provides this as a free service for those who don't have an online brokerage account. Whether through an online brokerage or through StockCharts.com you can build charts and incorporate one or more technical indicators of your choice into the charts to assist in analyzing the potential for short-term price directions. You can usually save the charts for future reference, updating any changes if desired.

"The charting features available for free on BigCharts.com (www.bigcharts.com) can also be very useful. There are many services that offer technical analysis through charting and commentary in greater detail for a fee, both over the Internet as well as published periodicals. Never has there been this level of data available to the individual investor to assist in timing decisions.

"I'd suggest you just jot these down as we go through them. Ready for the next one?" Max inquired.

"Ready...fire...aim!" Ernie countered.

MOVING AVERAGES

"OK. Let's talk about another very popular one—a 'moving average.' This one has been around for a long time. As technical indicators go, I think this is pretty useful. A moving average shows the trend in the *average* price of a stock or market index over a specific period of time. As the name indicates, the time period 'moves.' For example, moving averages usually make use of a 10, 30, 50, 100, or 200 day calculation period, depending on the whims of the user. The longer the time period, the more the average gets smoothed out. And, when a new day is added, the last day drops off. So, if you were calculating a 50 day moving average for a stock, you would take the price--usually the closing price--at the end of each of these fifty consecutive trading days, add them all up, and divide by fifty. That would be the moving average for the first point on your chart. The next day you would add the closing price for that day and delete the first day's price, make the same calculation for the second point, and so on. Make sense?"

"Yes, I see," Karie responded. "But what do you do with that information?"

"Well, over time you will have a line that will develop based on these average prices. Now here's the key. If the moving average line is moving in an upward direction and the current price of the stock crosses above the moving average, then a buy signal may be indicated. Conversely, if the moving average is moving in a downward direction and the current price crosses below the moving average, it may be generating a sell signal. Again, there's no assurance that either of these would be the case, so technicians usually give consideration to other indicators as well to strengthen their case.

"A different twist on this would be a 'weighted moving average.' This is calculated in the same way as what we just discussed, except that a higher weight is assigned to the most recent day and a progressively lesser weight to previous days. For example, if you were calculating a 10 day moving average, you would multiply the closing price on the first day by 1, the closing price on the second day by 2, and so on until you multiply the tenth day price by 10. You would add up all of these numbers and divide by the sum of the weights. This would give you a weighted moving average. In this case, a simple upward or downward turn in this average is believed to indicate a buy or sell signal.

"These potential buy or sell signals...they pertain to the stocks and not to the call options we sell, right?" Ernie asked.

"Correct. However, as we discussed a bit ago, if you believed your indicators were predicting an increase or decrease in the price of a stock you own, you could use that information to your advantage in deciding *when* you write your calls, the *strike price* at which you write them, and perhaps also the *expiration date* that would make the most sense. Do you see what I mean?"

"Yes, I do. But what if an indicator turns out to be some kind of false signal?"

"That's a great question. Such a risk is certainly there. And that's why investors who use technical analysis usually take a number of indicators into consideration to see if most are pointing in the same direction. If there is no pattern developing, it might be best just to ignore them and go solely with your fundamental analysis."

RELATIVE STRENGTH INDEX (RSI)

"Here's another one that seems to have some merit," Max continued. "The 'Relative Strength Index (RSI)' measures the momentum of a stock's price in relationship to itself. Take good notes on this one, as it's a little more complicated. RSI measures the closing average of a stock's up days divided by the closing average of the stock's down days. So, as you are keeping track of the closing prices, you would also need to indicate a '+' next to a day when the closing price is higher than the previous trading day and a '-' when the price is lower. I like to use a 30 day measurement period. After you have a series of 30 days of prices, you would do the following:

(1) Add the closing prices for the up days and divide the total by 30
(2) Add the closing prices for the down days and divide the total by 30
(3) Divide the up day average from step 1 by the down day average from step 2
(4) Then add 1 to the result from step 3
(5) Divide 100 by the number arrived at in step 4
(6) Subtract the number arrived at in step 5 from 100

"This process would continue in the same way a moving average is calculated.

"Is that really supposed to make any sense?" Karie asked in astonishment.

"Only if it works!" Ernie quipped. ""You can see why using the charting services available from your online brokerage or these other sources are absolutely necessary unless you want to spend all day crunching numbers. Here's the significance of the RSI calculation. After computing these six steps, a signal to buy a stock is said to be triggered when the resulting number is in the area of 30. Correspondingly, a sell signal is supposed to occur when the number is in the area of 70. And remember--this indicator should not be used in isolation. It should be used with other indicators to see if trend signals are developing."

UPSIDE DOWNSIDE RATIO

"While the indicators we've discussed so far could be used for broad market averages as well, I find them most useful for individual stocks. This next one, however, is intended as a broad indicator of market direction in general. It takes the volume of New York Stock Exchange stocks that are advancing and divides this by the volume of New York Stock Exchange stocks that are declining. This information is available in many of the daily financial newspapers and probably on some Internet Web sites as well. A moving average of 10 to 20 days should be used, calculated as we've previously discussed. A result above 4 is thought to be a positive buy signal and a result below .75 is thought to be a negative sell signal.

"There are many other indicators such as 'Bollinger Bands,' 'Stochastics,' the 'ARMS Short-Term Trading Index,' 'Put/Call Ratio,' and on and on. You could look these up at the library or online using a search engine and use them if they make sense to you. I think this is a good point to stop though. These kinds of things can go on forever, and we don't want to get caught up in 'analysis paralysis.'

"I think my brain is currently in paralysis," Karie admitted.

"Well, please keep in mind that you don't have to use technical analysis at all in order to be successful at covered call writing. But if you decide to pursue using it, you may end up with even better investment returns. And your success in meeting and even exceeding your investment return objectives is what this has been all about."

Max slumped back into his chair, closed his eyes momentarily, and took the longest pause since the sessions had started.

"That's the end of the course, folks," Max announced with a deep sigh. "How did I do?"

Karie jumped up from her chair, ran over to Max and gave him a big hug. "You've done exquisitely, Max, because even I understand this."

"I do too, Max," Ernie echoed. "And don't ever be shy about being called a guru. I looked up the definition of the word last week and found that it means 'Dispeller of Darkness' in Sanskrit. That's what you truly are, Max. You've shed a lot of light on this whole subject of covered call writing for us. In fact, you can consider it fully demystified. You've helped make our retirement dream a reality!"

Max, The Guru, tired and slightly red-faced, was beaming.

"Since you hung in there with me and completed the 'course,' I should probably give you a diploma…or at least a certificate of attendance," Max joked. "But instead of that, I'm going to just give you a 'guide' that lists everything an investor needs to remember from start to finish to get ready for and to successfully carry out a program of covered call option writing. Follow this and nothing should ever fall between the cracks.

"There," The Guru announced. "That was my commencement address!"

(For you, Reader/Investor, you will find "A Guide For Covered Call Option Writing" located in the Appendix, a quiz and answer key.)

PRACTICAL APPLICATIONS FOR MAKING MONEY

Consider the economic scenarios described in this chapter. Try to determine which scenario the economy is in at this time. Refer back to the information in the chapter if needed:

( ) Peak in inflation and interest rates
( ) Falling inflation and interest rates
( ) Increasing inflation and interest rates
( ) Slowing economy

After you have selected the scenario, try to determine where *within* the scenario the economy is and the direction it is moving (admitting that this is only an informed guess).

Based on your feelings about the above, what action would you likely take regarding stock ownership and covered call writing? Select as many as apply:

( ) Sell stocks in these sectors: ______________________

____

( ) Buy stocks in these sectors: ______________________

____

( ) Write in-the-money calls
( ) Write out-of-the-money calls
( ) Avoid writing calls in anticipation of a rise in the market

14

READY...AIM...WRITE

> The more I practice, the
> luckier I get.
>
> Lee Trevino (by way of
> Thomas Jefferson)

Ernie called The Guru's assistant and set up one last Friday appointment...just for a brief period of time to go over a few things.

When Karie and Ernie arrived, Max was as busy as always, but happy to take time for them. Karie and Ernie had something important to tell Max, but in his usual fashion, he just started in where he had finished off. Rather than interrupt him, they let him pontificate.

FOR PRACTICE OR FOR REAL

"Glad to see you two," he said. "Now that we're done you will soon be off and running with this. You've got the tools you need to do business as covered call writing investors and to stick to it. But you don't have to jump in with both feet. In fact, you don't have to jump in with any feet at all at first if you don't want to.

"It is very easy to take this program and use it simply on paper until you are comfortable with it. You can use Zacks and Value Line for hypothetical stock selections. You can use your online brokerage account to select a portfolio of hypothetical call writing opportunities with the assistance of the Excel 'calls' template. You can watch the action as your friend Father Time passes through options expirations and you write new hypothetical calls, and you can use the 'results' template to keep track of what you are doing. How does that sound to you?" Max inquired.

Karie and Ernie could hardly contain themselves.

"Max," Ernie finally broke in. "Karie and I spent a lot of time talking over all of this since our last meeting. First, we both want to thank you so much for all of the important information you have shared with us and the time you have been willing to give to us. It will make a big difference in our retirement lives!

"Since we met last, we've been approved for covered call writing through our discount broker…and we decided to go ahead and do some trades on a few of the stocks we already own. We used the 'calls' template you gave us, and it worked beautifully. We looked at a lot of alternatives, and the template helped us make some very informed decisions about which strike prices and expirations to use to achieve our investment return objective. So…in short, we are already on the road. And we know what road we're on, so we will get there. We know now that we can achieve our investment objective using what you have taught us. Our first set of covered call option writing trades are giving us an annualized yield of over twelve-percent, with opportunity for additional capital appreciation."

Max was surprised and very pleased at how quickly Ernie and Karie had acted. They had really taken his advice to heart. With a lot of review and some practice, they were obviously very comfortable already with the decision making and the mechanical processes of writing covered call options.

"Well, it sounds to me like you are the gurus now!" Max said with a big smile.

"No, Max," Ernie responded. "You will always be The Guru. But there's more that we want to tell you. We've just written over $20,000 in call premiums. And, as you said, the broker has already put the premium income in our accounts. We took that income and reinvested it in a new stock that fits into our portfolio beautifully. Then we wrote more call options on the new stock, giving us even more premium income and now that cash is already in our account too!"

"Yes," Karie interjected. "We knew we didn't want to use leverage through buying stocks on margin. We figure that using some of our premium income to buy more stocks and then write more options on the stock bought with the option income is our best way to obtain leverage and continue to build our portfolio."

Max was truly delighted by how far Ernie and Karie had come in their thinking, and acting, on what he had taught them. For the first time Max was momentarily at a loss for words.

Karie continued. "And we took a really hard look at the research on Triple-O Internet Services. We still believe in the company's future prospects, at least at this time. We did decide, however, to write options on it. We looked up some of the other strike prices and expirations and decided to go with the $50 strike price and an option that will expire in about 6 months from now. We just couldn't pass up the opportunity to lock in greater than a 24% return on the option contracts. If it goes down from here, we've got almost

$6 ½ per share of downside protection from the premium income."

"It sounds like a great investment decision," Max acknowledged to both of them. "But what if the stock skyrockets and goes way beyond the strike price? Just about anything can happen in six months."

"We talked about that," Ernie responded, "and noted that we would be achieving our maximum investment return goal we calculated when the option contracts were written. With retirement coming up our circumstances and investment objectives are changing. While we continue to like the stock, we are willing to accept the volatility and the downside risk on it. And of course we would be protected somewhat by the call premium income. If the stock shoots upward and gets called away, we will likely use the money to further diversify our stock holdings and start writing more call options."

Both Karie and Ernie grinned and Karie said, "We are now in the business of writing covered call options on our stock investments, Max...and we're sticking to it!"

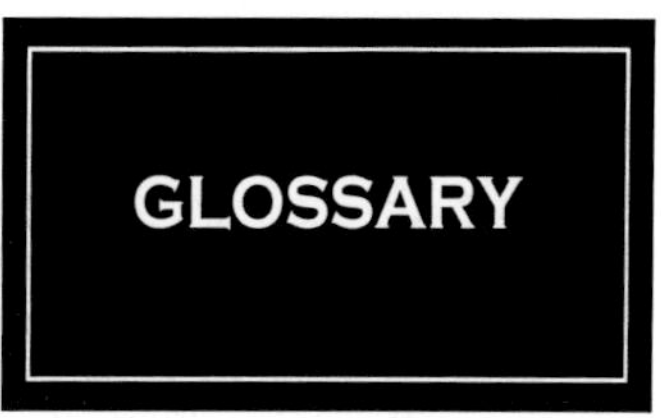

GLOSSARY

ALL-OR-NONE ORDER – A type of limit order which directs a broker to either fill the entire order or, if it cannot be filled, to fill none of it.

ASK – The price offered by an owner to sell a security, such as a stock or an option.

ASSIGNED – The requirement by the writer of an option to perform according to the terms of the contract by making delivery of the underlying stock to the holder (buyer) of the option through a sale. This is done by the option writer's broker. The stock is also said to have been "called away."

AT-THE-MONEY – The strike price and the market price of the underlying stock are exactly equal or very close.

BETA – A mathematical measure of price sensitivity and volatility for a given stock compared with the market as a whole. A beta greater than 1.0 indicates higher price volatility. Conversely, a beta of under 1.0 implies lower price volatility than the market in general. Generally high beta stocks perform well in a strong bull market but underperform in a bear market.

BID – The price offered by a buyer to purchase a security, such as a stock or option.

BUY TO CLOSE – The placing of an order by an option writer to buy back the option in order to close out the position.

CALL – An option permitting the holder (buyer) to purchase a stock at a predetermined price until a certain date. For example, an investor may purchase a call option on XYZ stock giving the investor the right to buy 100 shares (for each option contract) at $50 per share until June 15.

CAPITAL APPRECIATION – An increase in the market value of a security.

CAPITAL DEPRECIATION – A decrease in the market value of a security.

CAPITAL GAIN – Occurs when the proceeds from a stock or an option sale is greater than its cost. When writing covered calls, for example, if you receive $3 per share in premium income and the calls expire worthless, your cost is $0 per share and the capital gain is $3 per share.

CAPITAL LOSS – Occurs when the proceeds from a stock or an option sale is less than its cost. When writing covered calls, for example, if you receive $3 per share in premium income and you buy back the calls at $4, the capital loss is $1 per share.

COVERED – Implies that the investor who writes a call option owns the underlying stock, so that if the stock is assigned the writer has the stock to deliver to the call holder (buyer).

COVERED CALL OPTION WRITING – An investment program for stock owners who are generally seeking a conservative way to increase income from their shares by selling (writing) calls on the stock they own. There is also the opportunity for a defined amount of capital appreciation in the stock (for out-of-the-money calls) and the stock owner receives any dividends. The option writer receives premium income in exchange for assuring that the buyer of the option can purchase the shares at the agreed strike price during the operative time period of the option contract.

DAY ORDER – An order to buy or sell a security that will expire at the end of the day the order is placed if it is not executed.

DOLLAR COST AVERAGING – Investment of money at regular or periodic intervals. This results in purchasing more shares during a down market and fewer shares during a rising market. Those who use dollar cost averaging believe that the price of the security they are purchasing will rise over the long term, but that it is not possible to know exactly when to buy it at the best price all at once.

EXCHANGE TRADED FUND (ETF) - ETFs represent shares of ownership in portfolios of common stocks which are designed to generally correspond to the price and yield performance of their underlying portfolios of securities, either broad market, industry sectors, regions, investment styles or international. ETFs give investors the opportunity to buy or sell an entire portfolio of stocks within a single security, as easily as buying or selling a share of stock. They offer a wide range of investment opportunities.

EXERCISE – In the case of covered call options, to require delivery of the underlying stock by the seller (writer) of the options to the holder (buyer).

EXPIRATION DATE – The last day an option holder (buyer) can exercise the rights in an option contract.

FUNDAMENTAL ANALYSIS – A decision making process for stock selection or retention that is based on such factors as a company's earnings, examination of financial statements and the quality of its management.

FUNGIBLE – Relates to assets that are identical and are interchangeable. For example, shares of General Electric common stock or the April $30 General Electric calls are both fungible. All General Electric common stock shares are the same and are interchangeable and all of the General Electric April $30 call contracts are the same and are interchangeable.

GOOD-'TIL-CANCELED ORDER (GTC) – An order to buy or sell a security that remains in force until it is executed or canceled.

INSTITUTIONAL INVESTOR – Large investors in the securities markets such as mutual funds, bank trust departments, insurance companies, brokerage firms and pension funds. Many institutional investors use covered call writing as one of their investment strategies.

IN-THE-MONEY – The strike price of a call option is below the market price of the underlying stock. For example, the call option for a stock with a strike price of $50 when the stock is trading at $52 would be $2 in-the-money.

INTRINSIC VALUE – That part of an option's market price which is in-the-money. For example, if the current market price of an option is $3 ½ and the option is in-the-money by $2, the intrinsic value is $2 and the time value is $1 ½. If an option is at-the-money or out-of-the-money there is no intrinsic value.

INVERTED (NEGATIVE) YIELD CURVE – A condition where yields (investment returns) on long-term bonds are lower than interest rates on short-term bonds. "Inverted" or "negative" refers to the downward slope when drawing a graph with the vertical axis representing yield/rate and the horizontal axis representing time to maturity of the bond. The opposite condition would be a "positive yield curve."

LEAPS – An acronym for Long-Term Equity Anticipation Securities. These are options with expiration dates extending up to three years, which is well beyond the term of regular options.

LEVERAGE – An attempt by an investor to increase the rate of return from an investment by assuming additional risk.

Examples of leverage would be buying securities on margin and speculating by purchasing options.

LIMIT ORDER – An order to execute a transaction only at a specified limit price or better. Investors would use a limit order to establish a price at which they are willing to trade.

LIMIT PRICE – The price specified by an investor for a limit order. For an order to write covered calls, this represents the lowest price the investor will accept.

LONG-TERM – Relates to the gain or loss in a security that has been held for a certain period of time. For example, to qualify as a long-term capital gain under current tax laws, a security must be held for twelve months or more.

MARGIN (ACCOUNT) – A feature of a brokerage account which permits an investor to borrow funds through the broker to purchase additional securities, thus providing investment leverage.

MARGIN CALL – A call by the broker for additional funds or securities to be added to the margin account when the value of the equity in the account has declined below minimum requirements.

MARKET ORDER – An order for immediate execution at the best price available when the order reaches the exchange.

MOVING AVERAGE – A technical indicator used in technical analysis to predict trends in stock prices. This indicator is represented by a rolling series of successive average numbers for a defined period of time (typically 10, 30, 50, 100 or 200 days). When a new number is added, the oldest number is dropped from the average.

ODD LOT – Refers to fewer than 100 shares of common stock.

OPTION – A contract permitting the holder (buyer) to purchase (call) or sell (put) a stock at a fixed price (strike) until a specific date (expiration).

OPTION AGREEMENT – A written document that must be signed by an option investor and given to the brokerage company before the investor may be approved for trading in options. The purpose of the agreement is to help assure that the investor has adequate knowledge (such as the knowledge contained in this book in the case of covered calls) and that the investor's goals are appropriate for the type of option transactions the investor is asking the brokerage company to provide. The investor is also supplied with a copy of *Characteristics and Risks of Standardized Options*.

OPTION CHAIN – A string of option quotes for a specific stock which includes every expiration date and strike price available for options on that stock. This is typically provided by online brokers as a part of their automated quotation service to simplify the identification of ticker symbols for options and to facilitate obtaining quotes and executing trades.

OPTION CONTRACT – An agreement by an option writer to sell a given stock at a predetermined price (strike) until a certain date (expiration). The holder (buyer) of the option is not obligated to exercise (act on) the option, but the seller (writer) of the option must perform the obligation if the buyer exercises rights under the option contract.

OPTION CYCLE – Each stock is given a series of up to four months during which option contracts expire. Options for a stock generally expire on the same four months every year, plus the current month and the next following month.

OPTIONS CLEARING CORPORATION – Referred to as the OCC, it is an organization established in 1972 to process and guarantee options transactions that take place on the organized exchanges.

ORDINARY INCOME – Income from sources such as wages, dividends and interest. These items of income do not qualify for special tax treatment. Short-term capital gains are also taxed as ordinary income.

OUT-OF-THE-MONEY - The strike price of a call option is above the market price of the underlying stock. For example, the call option for a stock with a strike price of $55 when the stock is trading at $52 would be $3 out-of-the-money.

POSITIVE YIELD CURVE – A condition where yields (investment returns) on long-term bonds are greater than interest rates on short-term bonds. "Positive" refers to the upward slope when drawing a graph with the vertical axis representing yield/rate and the horizontal axis representing time to maturity of the bond. The opposite condition would be an "inverted (negative) yield curve."

PREMIUM – The current price at which an option contract trades and the amount a buyer would pay and a seller would receive. The amount of the premium is determined by a variety of factors, including the time remaining to expiration, the strike price chosen, the price and beta of the underlying stock, and interest rates.

PRICE/EARNINGS (P/E) RATIO – This ratio is computed by dividing the price of a stock by its current (or sometimes its projected) earnings per share.

PUT - An option permitting the holder (buyer) to sell a stock at a predetermined price until a certain date. For example, an investor may purchase a put option on General Electric stock giving the investor the right to sell 100 shares (for each option contract) at $20 per share until June 15.

RESISTANCE – A price level for a stock or a market at which it is believed the supply for stock will increase relative to the demand based upon historical precedence and therefore the price will decline.

ROLLING DOWN – Buying back a call option position and then writing a new call with the same maturity, but with a lower strike price.

ROLLING FORWARD – Buying back a call option position and then writing a new call at the same strike price, but with a longer expiration.

ROLLING UP – Buying back a call option position and then writing a new call with the same maturity, but with a higher strike price.

ROUND LOT - For common stocks the standard unit of trading is a round lot, which is 100 shares or a multiple thereof.

SECURITIES AND EXCHANGE COMMISSION (SEC) - The federal agency that administers securities laws in the United States. The SEC, created under the Securities Exchange Act of 1934, governs the following: registration of organized securities exchanges, proxy solicitation, disclosure requirements for securities in the secondary market and regulation of insider trading. This Act, along with the Securities Act of 1933, forms the basis of securities regulation.

SELL-TO-OPEN - The placing of an initial order by an option writer to sell an option in order to establish a position. The writer receives premium income from the buyer of the option. (Also referred to as "sell covered call.")

SHORT-TERM – Relates to the gain or loss in a security that has been held for a certain period of time. For example, under current tax laws the gain or loss in a security held for less than one year would be short-term.

SHORT POSITION – An investment position where the investor has written an option with the contract obligation remaining outstanding.

STRIKE PRICE – The price at which the holder (buyer) of a call option can purchase the underlying stock. Also sometimes referred to as the "exercise price."

SUPPORT – A price level for a stock or a market at which it is believed the demand for stock will increase relative to the supply based upon historical precedence and therefore the price will increase.

TECHNICAL ANALYSIS – A decision making process for stock selection or retention that is based on the interrelationships between a group of elements relating to a company's securities, such as price level, price movement, volume of trading, and perhaps other factors. It deals only with perceived demand and supply issues relating to a company's securities.

TECHNICAL INDICATOR – A variable developed from technical analysis that is believed to be a predictor of which stocks to invest in and the timing for selection. Examples of such indicators are support and resistance levels, moving averages, relative strength, Bollinger Bands, Stochastics, the ARMS Short-Term Trading Index, Put/Call Ratio, and others.

TICKER SYMBOL – The abbreviation for a stock or option used on securities quotation machines. For example, "GE" is the stock ticker symbol for General Electric and "GEFG" is the option ticker symbol for General Electric calls with a June expiration and a strike price of $35.

TIME VALUE - That part of an option's market price which is solely attributable to the remaining time before the expiration of the option. If the option is out-of-the-money or at-the-money, the entire premium is attributable to time value. If the option is in-the-money, the amount attributable to time value is calculated by subtracting the amount by which the option is in-the-money from the current option premium. For example, if the current market price of an option is $3 ½ and the option is in-the-money by $2, the time value is $1 ½.

UNCOVERED (NAKED) – Implies that the investor who writes a call option does not own the underlying stock, so that if the stock is assigned the writer must purchase shares at the current market price to deliver to the call holder (buyer). Also known as "naked" because, if the option is exercised, the writer is without shares and is caught naked. If the stock subject to the call rises significantly, the writer could be exposed to substantial (theoretically unlimited) losses. This is an extremely high-risk strategy, even more speculative than buying calls.

UNDERLYING STOCK – The stock owned by the option writer that the option holder (buyer) has the right, but not the obligation, to purchase according to the terms of the option contract.

UNREALIZED GAIN – Occurs when the value of an unsold asset rises above its original cost. Also referred to as a "paper gain."

UNREALIZED LOSS – Occurs when the value of an unsold asset is reduced below its original cost. Also referred to as a "paper loss."

WRITING CALLS – Another term for selling covered call contracts on stock an investor owns.

The following support material has been added, which may be of little or considerable use to the Reader/Investor, depending on personal experience with investing in general and the use of options in particular:

A SUMMARY OF THE BENEFITS AND FEATURES OF COVERED CALL OPTION WRITING

The following is a summary of some of the benefits, features and characteristics of writing covered call options and the reasons why you as an investor should consider making it your business to use them:

1. **Additional income** – Writing covered call options can provide you with an ongoing stream of premium income from your stocks. This is particularly important at a time when most common stocks either pay no dividend at all or provide a very meager return on investment. The premium income can also significantly enhance total returns in a slower growth stock market.

2. **Income paid up front** - The premium received from call writing options is credited to your account the next day, creating immediate cash flow that can be reinvested to produce more income or can be withdrawn from your brokerage account for any use. Since the premium income is paid up front, if the funds are reinvested it can enhance the overall yield on the original investment.

3. **Predetermined return** – The immediate and annualized returns from call option writing can all be evaluated prior to initiating the position. You will know what the

premium income will be and the maximum additional capital appreciation opportunity if your stock is called away at the strike price.

4. **Risk reduction** - If a stock declines, the premium you received helps to offset some, or all, of the decline in stock value. Writing covered calls acts like an insurance policy offering some downside protection when a stock declines in price.

5. **Cash dividends** – Since you, as an option writer, own the stock and have only sold an option, you will continue to be entitled to any cash dividends until exercise.

6. **Fungibility** – Exchange-listed options are fungible. That is, each listed option with a common expiration date and exercise price is interchangeable with any similar listed option. This enables investors to initiate and close out a position by simply reversing the transaction (buying to close) in the open market through their brokerage account. Fungible option contracts became available in 1973.

7. **Ease of trading** - Since options are actively traded on the open market, call options can be easily written and bought back, similar to trading stocks. With the assistance of this book, it is readily accomplished yourself with online or phone trading through a discount brokerage account.

8. **Diversification of stocks for option writing** - There are a huge number of stocks within a broad array of industry

groups from which to choose for covered call writing opportunities. Some of the stocks pay large dividends while some pay none at all. Exchange Traded Funds that achieve broad diversification by mirroring large portfolios of stocks are becoming more and more available. Writing covered calls is possible on some of these ETFs and will likely become more widely available in the future.

9. **Diversification of expiration dates and exercise prices –** Options usually have four or more possible expiration dates to choose from. In addition, LEAPS (Long-term Equity Anticipation Securities, which are options on selected underlying stocks with expirations of up to three years at the time of listing) are also available on many stocks.

10. **Cash or margin account -** Covered call options may be written either in a cash or a margin account (cash only for retirement accounts).

11. **Options listed in daily newspapers, brokerages, and online -** A table of actively traded listed options, their expirations, their exercise prices, and their closing prices from the previous day is available on a current basis in most daily newspapers. A detailed quote for any option is always available through online brokerage accounts. Many brokerages also have automated quotation systems for customer use over the phone. Extensive online options quotations are also available through the Yahoo! Finance section (www.yahoo.com) and other Internet sources.

A SUMMARY OF THE RISKS OF COVERED CALL OPTION WRITING

The following is a summary of the risks of writing covered call options for the investor:

1. **Investing in the stock market** – Writing covered call options requires that the investor own stocks or Exchange Traded Funds, which are stock market investments that are subject to market risk. Writing covered calls, however, provides some downside protection in declining markets. Therefore, the investor in stocks or Exchange Traded Funds on which covered call options have been written is always better off than the investor who owns the same stocks but does not write covered call options if the stocks decline in value.

2. **Limited stock gains in a rising market** – An option writer's potential gain is limited to the amount of premium income received plus any gain in the price of the underlying stock from the time the option was written up to the dollar amount of the strike price. Depending on the strike price and the extent of a rise in the underlying stock prior to expiration, in a rapidly rising market the option writer would not benefit from all of the rise in a stock if it appreciates more than the combination of the above two gains. Approximately eighty-percent of options that are out-of-the-money when written expire unexercised, and

therefore worthless (a positive occurrence for the covered call option writer compared with the stock owner who does not write options). Nonetheless, an option writer faces the risk that it might have been better financially to have simply held the stock and not written covered call options in a rapidly rising market.

3. **Unanticipated exercise of options** – The holder (buyer) of a call option has the right, but not the obligation, to buy (exercise) the option writer's stock at the strike price at any time through the expiration date. A writer can expect that his stock will rarely be subject to exercise if the market price of the stock is less than the strike price of the call option written. If, however, the market price rises above the strike price, it is possible that the holder could exercise the call option at any time, thus requiring the option writer to sell the underlying stock at the strike price. Exercise of options generally occurs at the expiration date, and then usually only if the market price exceeds the strike price. On occasion, however, a holder will exercise an option prior to the expiration date. This is beneficial in some respects for the option writer, as the writer is paid the strike price early and can decide how to deploy the funds immediately instead of having to wait until the expiration date. A potential negative for the writer would be if the stock on which options have been written is highly appreciated stock. This would mean that when the holder exercises the option, a substantial capital gain is triggered on which taxes must be paid by the writer. The writer may have planned a strategy of rolling forward or rolling up to defer the potential capital gain tax. However, the unanticipated exercise of the option by

the holder means that the writer is not able to carry out the strategy and would be locked into the tax consequences from the capital gain unless new shares are immediately purchased in substitute to deliver to the call option holder.

4. **Potential lack of option market liquidity** – Option contracts generally trade in much smaller quantities than common stock shares. Options for some stocks are very actively traded. For other, less well-followed stocks, there are usually fewer option contracts traded. This may cause the bid and ask price spread to widen significantly. For this reason, investors are encouraged to always place limit orders with their brokers on option trades instead of market orders to eliminate the risk of an order being filled at a different price than what a current quote might indicate.

5. **Possibility of a decrease in option premiums** – The price of option premiums is determined by market forces and mathematical models. During periods of market volatility, option premiums tend to be greater than during periods of stable markets. It is not possible to predict future volatility. Should markets become less volatile, or should markets be less attractive to investors in the future, it is possible that option premiums may not be as large as they have been in the past. Such an occurrence would tend to make the returns on covered call writing less attractive than they have been during periods of larger option premiums.

6. **Relatively higher cost of option trades** – The commissions charged by full-service brokers and discount brokers vary significantly. Overall, however, the cost to the investor for option trades generally tends to be higher than for stock trades considering the amount of money involved in the trades. It is important to the investor to find a discount brokerage where commission costs can be reasonably managed.

A GUIDE FOR COVERED CALL OPTION WRITING

For investors who wish to use covered call option writing as an investment strategy, this guide will assure that all appropriate steps have been taken in the proper order:

STEP 1:

SELF-EDUCATION ON COMMON STOCK SELECTION

The following books and Web sites are recommended for investors to be used as needed for educational purposes:

Beginning Investors: *The Wall Street Journal Guide To Understanding Money & Investing;* www.motleyfool.com

All Investors: *Beating The Street;* www.marketwatch.com; www.cnbc.com; www.briefing.com

Seasoned Investors: *Stocks For The Long Run;* www.investors.com; www.wsj.com

STEP 2:

ESTABLISHING A BROKERAGE ACCOUNT

Due to lower commission costs, it is recommended that investors select a discount brokerage account and trade online or on the telephone. Fidelity and Charles Schwab are suggested for consideration due to their size, support capabilities and offerings of complete cash management accounts.

Action required: select and open account; obtain approval from brokerage to trade covered call options

Major discount brokers include:

Fidelity Investments: www.fidelity.com; 800-544-5555

Charles Schwab & Co.: www.schwab.com; 800-2-SCHWAB

Accutrade: www.accutrade.com; 800-494-8939

Ameritrade: www.ameritrade.com; 800-454-9272

Harris Direct: www.harrisdirect.com; 800-825-5723

E-Trade: www.etrade.com; 800-ETRADE1

Scottrade: www.scottrade.com; 800-619-SAVE

TD Waterhouse: www.tdwaterhouse.com; 800-TDWATERHOUSE

STEP 3:

SUBSCRIPTION TO INVESTMENT ADVISORY SERVICE

If individual stocks will be purchased, investors may wish to subscribe to an advisory service. Such a service will not only provide stock purchase recommendations of its own, but also provide the investor with a resource for research on companies whose names are obtained from other sources.

Well-known investment advisory services to consider:

- Value Line Investment Survey: www.valueline.com; 800-634-3583
- Zacks Investment Research: www.zacksadvisor.com; 800-767-3771

STEP 4:

ESTABLISH LIST OF PROSPECTIVE STOCKS TO PURCHASE

Individual Stocks: For individual stocks, select up to twenty company names that will assure adequate diversification to minimize risk. Maintain the list over time by researching these and other names so that an ongoing list of stocks to fit the portfolio objectives is ready and current as cash becomes available for reinvestment. Use the brokerage account to determine whether options are available for all stocks on the list.

Exchange Traded Funds: For ETFs, utilize www.amex.com as a resource for determining what funds are available. Use your favorite search engine to find Web pages on "Exchange Traded Funds" or "ETF," which will provide links that may yield information on new and existing funds. Formulate a list of broad based and industry sector ETF funds that fit the portfolio objectives. Use the brokerage account to determine whether options are available for ETFs on the list.

STEP 5:

USE EXCEL TEMPLATE ("CALLS") OR MANUAL WORKSHEET ("OPPORTUNITIES")

Using the discount brokerage account, obtain and enter the required data onto the Excel "calls" worksheet or the manual worksheet for the diversified individual stocks and/or Exchange Traded Funds in the above lists to provide yield and other information. Select at least several examples of various expiration dates and strike prices for each.

STEP 6:

REVIEW "CALLS" WORKSHEET OR MANUAL WORKSHEET DATA AND MAKE OPTION WRITING SELECTIONS

Print out the "calls" worksheet and review the data or the manual worksheet data to make specific selections of option writing opportunities that will provide diversification in stock selection (industries represented in the portfolio), provide call option diversification (expiration and strike price), and will provide the overall targeted yield.

STEP 7:

INITIATE STOCK TRADES

Initiate stock purchase ("buy") trades with the discount broker based on final decisions as determined by the review. Verify that orders have been filled.

STEP 8:

INITIATE OPTION TRADES

Initiate call option writing ("sell-to-open," also known as "sell covered call") trades with the discount broker based on final decisions as determined by the review. Verify that orders have been filled. Consider how to invest or use the premium income deposited into your account the next day after trades are filled.

STEP 9:

USE EXCEL TEMPLATE ("RESULTS") OR MANUAL WORKSHEET ("TRANSACTIONS")

From the discount brokerage account confirmations (either hard copy or online), enter the required data onto the Excel "results" worksheet (use the "Trade Sort" tab) or the manual worksheet as a permanent record of covered call writing trades. Copy and paste this data into other tabs on the worksheet and sort, as desired.

STEP 10:

FOR STOCKS SOLD THROUGH ASSIGNMENT OF CALLS AT EXPIRATION

Go back to Step 4 and select new stocks when cash is received from sales of stock due to assignment of call options, or if stocks are sold for any other reason. Continue forward through the rest of the steps.

STEP 11:

FOR COVERED CALL OPTIONS THAT EXPIRE AND ARE NOT EXERCISED (STOCK IS NOT ASSIGNED)

Go back to Step 5 and enter data for individual stocks or Exchange Traded Funds when calls expire unexercised. Continue forward through the rest of the steps.

HOW TO DETERMINE THE SYMBOL FOR AN OPTION

The single best and fastest way to determine an option symbol is to look up the "option chain" for a stock through an online discount brokerage account (see Chapter 10 for details). You may also call your broker for the information. An option symbol may, however, be determined manually in many, but not all, cases.

Every option has a symbol assigned to it, just as every stock has a ticker symbol. An investor needs to know what the symbol is for an option in order to look up its latest price, bid and ask, volume of trades and other information, as well as to trade the option contract. The information given below will assist the option investor in determining the symbol for many, but not all, call options.

The option symbol consists of three components:

- The ticker symbol for the underlying stock (or in some cases, such as NASDAQ stocks and LEAPS, a substitute for it)

- A letter indicating the month in which the option expires, and

- A letter indicating the strike price of the option

(1) **Ticker Symbol** – This can be a bit more complicated than it would seem. Often an option symbol will begin with the same symbol as the stock. With the huge expansion in the option alternatives available to investors, however, it has been necessary to use other initial letters beyond just the ticker symbol of the underlying stock. For example, the General Electric calls for expiration in June began with "GE," the same symbol as the stock. The calls expiring a year from next January, however, began with the symbol "WG." There would be no way for the investor to know this without checking with a broker, either directly or online. Again, there are never more than five letters in an option symbol. Since the next to the last letter signifies the expiration and the last letter indicates the strike price, there is room for no more than three additional letters at the beginning. As all NASDAQ stock symbols contain four letters, the option symbol for NASDAQ stocks will always begin with a three-letter substitute for the underlying stock symbol. For example, the ticker symbol for Cisco Systems, which is listed on NASDAQ, is "CSCO," however some of the options begin with CWY and others begin with CYQ. Another example is Microsoft, NASDAQ symbol "MSFT." Some of the Microsoft options begin with MQF and others with MSQ. If this is confusing to you, welcome to the club.

(2) **Expiration Letter** – The next to the last letter in the option symbol signifies the expiration of the option according to the following schedule:

CALL OPTION EXPIRATION DATES AND STRIKE PRICES

MONTH	LETTER
January	A
February	B
March	C
April	D
May	E
June	F
July	G
August	H
September	I
October	J
November	K
December	L

(3)**Strike Price Letter** – The last letter in the option symbol signifies the strike price of the option according to the following schedule:

STRIKE PRICE	LETTER	STRIKE PRICE	LETTER
$ 5	A	$70	N
$10	B	$75	O
$15	C	$80	P
$20	D	$85	Q
$25	E	$90	R
$30	F	$95	S
$35	G	$00	T
$40	H	$7 ½	U

$45	I	$12 ½	V
$50	J	$17 ½	W
$55	K	$22 ½	X
$60	L	$27 ½	Y
$65	M	$32 ½	Z

Thus, for the Johnson & Johnson (stock symbol "JNJ") April $55 calls, the option symbol is JNJDK ("JNJ" is for the stock symbol, "D" is for the April calls, and "K" is for the $55 strike price.

The Wal-Mart (stock symbol "WMT") September $65 calls would have the symbol WMTIM ("WMT" is for the stock symbol, "I" is for the September calls, and "M" is for the $65 strike price).

Note that the symbol "T" would apply whether the price of a stock is $100, $200, $300, and so on.

On occasion you may find a stock which has a $37 ½, $42 ½, $47 ½ or a higher multiple of $2 ½ option contract available. As all of the letters of the alphabet are used for strike prices from $5 through $32 ½, these higher strike prices also use a letter that is used for another strike price. This can be confusing, and your broker should be contacted to be sure you have the proper symbol.

FINDING QUOTES FOR OPTIONS
WITH NO ONLINE BROKERAGE ACCOUNT

Many daily newspapers and financial newspapers provide option quotes, however, they are incomplete. *The*

Wall Street Journal, Barron's and *Investors Business Daily* each provide a limited number of closing quotes on some of the more actively traded options each day.

For those who have online access (many local libraries have computers and Internet connections if needed), a very broad array of option quotes can be obtained at no cost (with only 15-20 minute delay from real-time) through the Yahoo! Web site, www.yahoo.com and other Internet sources. After entering the Yahoo! Web site, click on "Finance." Then enter the stock ticker symbol for the underlying stock on which you wish to write options (e.g., WMT for Wal-Mart). On the box just to the right, click on the menu arrow and select "Options," then click on "Get." The next window displays choices for calls on the left-hand side of the page. Above the "Calls" box, click on the expiration date for calls on which you wish to obtain quotes. A table of quotes appears on call options available for the expiration date you have selected. The following information is displayed: option symbol, last trade, change, bid, ask, volume, open interest, and strike price. Even more information is available by clicking on any option symbol.

HOW TO USE THE MICROSOFT® EXCEL TEMPLATE "CALLS" TO CALCULATE COVERED CALL WRITING OPPORTUNITIES

The Excel template provided on the CD/ROM with this book is designed to make covered call writing calculations as simple as possible. Microsoft® Excel is needed to run this template. The template provided can only be used on a PC unless Mac users have file-sharing software or a newer version of Excel.

Follow these instructions to use the template:

(1) Place the CD into your CD drive. Start your Excel program and load the template (the file is named "calls") from the appropriate drive.

(2) You may wish to save the template on your hard drive and may do so by clicking on the word "File" in the upper left hand corner of the worksheet and then clicking on "Save As" when the menu drops down. In the "File name" type "calls" and designate the desired file directory, which will save it under the same file name as on the CD.

(3) Completing the worksheet:

Note that on the template there are groupings of three lines for each company. You probably won't need more than three lines for each stock on which you are seeking option writing opportunities. However, if you do, simply insert additional rows at the end of a set and copy more of the lines as needed (see your Excel program manual for details if you don't know how to do this).

In cell C1 is the formula "=today()." Do not change this, as this is needed to automatically calculate the number of days in column H.

You will see an "x" under some columns in row 2. This means that you need to supply information into these columns to complete the template.

Complete as follows:

Column A: Enter the stock ticker symbol for the company.

Column B: Enter the number of shares you own or are contemplating buying.

Column C: Enter the current price per share or your cost of the stock, which ever is the most meaningful to you to compute your yield. If you have owned the stock for a long time and it is worth more than you paid for it, you may wish to use the market value rather than your cost basis, as that will give you a more accurate yield based on current value.

Column E: Enter the dividend per share, if any, the company currently pays.

Column F: You will note that starting in cell number U6 there are numerous expiration dates. Enter the expiration date of the option under consideration by clicking on the appropriate date. Then click the "Copy" button, move the cursor to the appropriate cell in column F and click, then click the "Paste" button. The expiration date you desire will be transferred. Note: with the passage of time, you can add additional expiration dates at the bottom of the list and copy over ones that expire. Simply type in the appropriate expiration date for future use. Use the third Friday of the month for expiration dates. If the expiration date is February 15, 2008 you should type 2/15/2008.

Column G: Enter the strike price of the option.

Column I: Enter the option symbol for the option under consideration (note: see "How To Determine the Symbol for an Option" in this Appendix, obtain symbols from option chain data if you have an online brokerage account or by phoning your broker).

Column J: Enter the current price of the premium (this should be approximately the average between the current bid and ask prices, or perhaps a little less).

After entering this information, the rest of the data will be completed by the template for your review.

The template is currently configured so that no brokerage commissions are included in the calculations. If you would like to customize the template to factor in brokerage commissions on your option trade and stock trade calculations (when the stock is called away from you at expiration), it can be done very easily using your commission schedule.

Place your cursor in cell S4 on the Excel template. Typically commissions on option trades are charged at a flat dollar amount and then a certain dollar amount per contract traded. Enter the flat dollar amount that applies to your schedule in cell S4. Then enter the dollar amount per contract charge in cell S5. Finally, the assumption is made that you are trading through an online discount brokerage account. If that is the case, you are most likely paying a flat rate on your stock trades at least up to 1,000 shares. Enter the flat dollar amount of commission you are paying on your stock trades in cell T4.

If your commission schedule is figured on a different basis than that described here, simply convert it to approximate the above schedule. It is not critically important that the brokerage commissions be exact. It is a reasonably small factor in your return calculations. You may choose to ignore commissions entirely in your calculations, or try to get it as exact as possible. The choice is yours.

HOW TO USE A DISCOUNT BROKER WITHOUT A COMPUTER AND CALCULCATING COVERED CALL WRITING OPPORTUNITIES MANUALLY

If you do not access your discount broker online, everything in this book is still available to you. Instead of obtaining quotes and executing your trades online, you will need to do this by telephone...either through direct conversation with a representative of your discount brokerage or by using their automated service whereby you press numbers on your touch-tone phone. It is recommended that you use the automated voice response phone system rather than speaking with a representative when initiating trades, as commissions can be significantly lower. Be sure that the discount broker you are using or considering offers the touch-tone automated phone access.

You should request instructions from your broker on how to use their service, as brokerages operate their systems somewhat differently. You may wish to utilize a representative personally at first until you become more comfortable with using the automated voice response phone system. All quotes and trading capabilities that are offered through a discount broker's Web site are offered through their representatives and are typically offered through their touch-tone automated voice response phone system as well. Therefore, while this may be a bit more laborious than obtaining quotes and trading online, you have access to everything you need to carry out the strategies in this book.

Complete the manual calculation page ("OPPORTUNITIES") as described below. Sheets are included at the end of the book and may be removed and copied. By following these instructions, you can make the same accurate calculations that are made using the Excel template…but this way is more work.

Column (A): Enter the name of the company whose stock you own.

Column (B): Enter the stock ticker symbol for the company.

Column (C): Enter the number of shares you own or are contemplating buying.

Column (D): Enter the current price per share.

Column (E): Multiply Column (C) and Column (D).

Column (F): Enter the dividend per share the company currently pays.

Column (G): Enter the expiration date of the option under consideration.

Column (H): Enter the strike price of the option.

Column (I): Enter the number of days between today's date and the expiration date.

Column (J): Enter the option symbol for the option under consideration (note: see "How to Determine the Symbol for an Option" under this Appendix).

Column (K): Enter the current price for the premium (this should be approximately the average between the current bid and ask prices, or perhaps a little less).

Column (L): Multiply Column (C) by Column (K) (reduce the total by the projected commission cost if complete accuracy is desired in the calculations).

Column (M): Divide Column (L) by Column (I).
Column (N): Divide Column (L) by Column (E).
Column (O): Multiply Column (N) by 365/Column (I). Then, if the stock pays a dividend, divide Column (F) by Column (D) and add the result to the previous calculation.
Column (P): Subtract Column (D) from Column (H) and multiply the difference by Column (C) (reduce the total by the projected commission cost to sell the stock if complete accuracy is desired in the calculations).
Column (Q): Divide Column (P) by Column (E). Then multiply that result by 365/Column I. Then add that result to Column (O).

If you are placing your order with a live representative at your brokerage, it is important that you say the right things for the sake of efficiency and to be sure that you are stating the information correctly so no mistakes are made either by you or by your broker. Phone calls are typically recorded.

Let's say that you have 1,000 shares of Wal-Mart on which you wish to write calls. After analyzing your alternatives, you have decided to write ten contracts (remember, one call contract equals 100 shares) of the January 2004 calls with a strike price of $60. The price you would like to get is $3.50 per contract, so you will be placing a limit order. (You could place a market order, however, limit orders are usually recommended due to the wide spreads that often occur between bid and ask prices on options.) You can either specify "good for the day" or "good 'til canceled," as you prefer.

To place the above order you would say to your broker's representative something like, "I would like to sell-to-open ten contracts of the Wal-Mart January, 2004 $60 calls at a limit price of $3.50, good for the day."

HOW TO USE THE MICROSOFT® EXCEL TEMPLATE "RESULTS" TO TRACK YOUR OPTION WRITING TRANSACTIONS

The Excel template provided on the CD/ROM with this book is designed to make tracking of your covered call option writing program results as simple as possible. Microsoft® Excel is needed to run this template. The template provided can only be used on a PC unless Mac users have file-sharing software.

Follow these instructions to use the template:

(1) Place the CD into your CD drive. Start your Excel program and load the template (the file is named "results") from the appropriate drive.

(2) You may wish to save the template on your hard drive and may do so by clicking on the word "File" in the upper left hand corner of the worksheet and then clicking on "Save As" when the menu drops down. In the "File name" type "results" and designate the desired file directory, which will save it under the same file name as on the CD.

(3) Completing the worksheet:

You should begin by being sure that you are working with the "TRADE SORT" tab of the template, which is located in the lower left hand corner of the worksheet, as the data in this worksheet is used as input for the other tabs.

You will see an "x" under some columns in row 3. This means that you need to supply information into these columns to make the template work. New rows can be added by replicating the information into the appropriate cells.

Complete as follows:

Column A: Enter an abbreviation for the account type for this option transaction (i.e. you may wish to use "PERS" for a personal taxable account and "IRA" for an IRA account. Use whatever abbreviations are meaningful for you, as long as you are consistent.)

Column B: Enter the stock ticker symbol for the company.

Column C: Enter the number of shares on which options were written for this transaction.

Column D: Enter the price per share at the time the option transaction was initiated or your cost of the stock, which ever is the most meaningful to you, to compute your yield. If you have owned the stock for a long time and it is worth more than you paid for it, you may wish to use the market value rather than your cost basis, as that will give you a more accurate yield based on current value.

Column F: Enter the date that the option transaction took place (for example, if the date of the transaction was August 15, 2001 you should type in 8/15/2001.

Column G: You will note that starting in cell number P6 there are numerous expiration dates. Enter the expiration date for the option transaction by positioning the cursor on the appropriate expiration date in column P. Then click the "Copy" button, move the cursor to the appropriate cell in column G and click, then click the "Paste" button. The expiration date you desire will be transferred. Note: with the passage of time, you can add additional expiration dates at the bottom of the list and copy over ones that expire. Simply type in the appropriate expiration date for future use. Use the third Friday of the month for expiration dates. You can also simply type in the expiration date. If the expiration date is February 15, 2008 you should type in 2/15/2008.

Column H: Enter the strike price of the option.

Column J: Enter the option symbol for the option transaction.

Column K: Enter the price of the premium per contract received for the option transaction.

Column L: Enter the exact amount of premium income received as stated on the brokerage confirmation report for this option transaction. Note: If the options are bought to close prior to expiration, reduce the amount of the premium income received for this transaction by the cost to purchase the contracts as stated on the brokerage confirmation report.

Column M: If the underlying shares are assigned upon expiration, enter the total of any capital appreciation or depreciation in this column, either using your cost basis or the market value of the stock at the time the option transaction was initiated, as you deem appropriate.

After entering this information, the rest of the data will be completed by the template.

(4) Completing the other tabs on the worksheet:

If you desire, the information from the "Trade Sort" tab can be copied and pasted into one or more of the other tabs to view the information in different ways. The "Expiration Sort" tab will allow you to see the same information sorted by expiration date. The "Stock Sort" tab sorts the information by stock, regardless of which account it may be in. The "Account Sort" tab sorts the information by account.

Start by going to the "Trade Sort" template and highlight all of the data by placing the cursor in the upper left hand cell where your data starts.

Press down on your mouse button and drag the cursor to the right and down until it darkens all of the data cells on your worksheet.

Then let go of the mouse button and all of your data will be selected.

Now click on the "Copy" icon at the top and click on the tab at the bottom you wish to use. It will take you to that worksheet, which appears the same as the worksheet for "Trade Sort."

Point and click the cursor into the same cell address as the cell from which you copied the data. Then all you have to do is click on the "Paste" icon and all of the data you copied will be pasted into the new worksheet.

Each of the tabbed worksheets has been formatted so that they will sort according to what the tab says. All you need to do now is click on the word "Data" at the top. A drop down menu box will appear. Click on "Sort" and another drop down menu comes up. Just click on the "OK" box at the bottom and your data is sorted.

HOW TO TRACK YOUR OPTION WRITING TRANSACTIONS MANUALLY

Complete the manual calculation page ("TRANSACTIONS") as described below. Sheets are included at the end of the book and may be removed and copied. By following these instructions, you can develop the same transaction records that are created by using the Excel template…but this way is more work.

Column (A): Enter the name of the company whose stock you own.

Column (B): Enter the stock ticker symbol for the company.

Column (C): Enter the number of shares on which you have written options for this transaction.

Column (D): Enter the current price per share.

Column (E): Multiply Column (C) and Column (D).

Column (F): Enter the trade date of the option transaction.

Column (G): Enter the expiration date of the option.

Column (H): Enter the strike price of the option.

Column (I): Enter the number of days between the option transaction date and the expiration date.

Column (J): Enter the option symbol for the option written.

Column (K): Enter the premium price per contract for this transaction.

Column (L): Enter the exact amount of premium income received as stated on the brokerage confirmation report for this option transaction. Note: If the options are bought to close prior to expiration, reduce the amount of the premium income received for this transaction by the cost to purchase the contracts as stated on the brokerage confirmation report. **Column (M):** If the underlying stock is called away at expiration of the option, enter the total amount of gain or loss on the stock based upon the cost basis of the stock or the market value at the time the option was written, which ever you deem appropriate.

Column (N): Add Column (L) and Column (M).

Column (O): Divide Column (N) by Column (E) and multiply that figure by 365 divided by Column (I).

SUGGESTED READING

The following books are suggested as possible readings for individuals desiring to learn more about market basics, how markets work and stock selection:

THE WALL STREET JOURNAL GUIDE TO UNDER-STANDING MONEY & INVESTING by Kenneth M. Morris, Virginia B. Morris, Alan M. Siegel, August 1999, paperback, 160 pages. This handy fact-filled book initiates you into the mysteries of the financial pages...buying stocks, bonds, mutual funds, futures and options, spotting trends and evaluating companies. A good beginning level investment book. Currently available over the Internet through Amazon.com for $12.76.

ONLINE INVESTING: The Wall Street Journal Interactive Edition's Complete Guide to Becoming A Successful Internet Investor by Dave Pettit (Contributor), Rich Jaroslovsky, 1st edition, May 23, 2000, hardback, 342 pages. The editors of the online version of *The Wall Street Journal* have produced a comprehensive overview of the best Web sites and resources available to the online investor. It tells where to find the best interactive tools, online calculators, and worksheets for selecting stocks and mutual funds and for researching and charting investments. Many other financial topics are covered. Currently available over the Internet through Amazon.com for $20.00.

STOCKS FOR THE LONG RUN – The Definitive Guide to Financial Market Returns and Long-Term Investment Strategies by Jeremy J. Siegel, Professor of Finance-the Wharton School of the University of Pennsylvania, 1998, hard cover, 301 pages. Siegel's book is a comprehensive and highly readable history of the stock market that dramatically makes the case for long-term investing in stocks. It is probably the best comprehensive text available about the market. An excellent reference for seasoned investors and anyone else interested in how the market works. Currently available over the Internet through Amazon.com for $23.96.

SECURITY ANALYSIS: Principles and Techniques by Benjamin Graham, David L. Dodd, Signey Cottle, and Charles Tatham, 5th ed. New York: McGraw-Hill, hard cover, 1988. The classic 1934 edition. Described by *The Motley Fool* as the bible of fundamental analysis. Benjamin Graham is the father of conservative financial analysis. His text is a classic that employs many of the investment theories practiced by Warren Buffett. Currently available over the Internet through Amazon.com for $40.

BEATING THE STREET by Peter Lynch, Simon & Schuster, 1993, hard cover, 318 pages. The author was manager of the highly successful Fidelity Magellan Fund for thirteen years until his retirement in 1990. In this book, Lynch shows investors how he puts his investing philosophy and techniques into action as he takes readers through the process of selecting the stocks he has recommended. Currently available over the Internet through Amazon.com for $11.20.

Note: Books are available in used condition from time to time through Amazon.com at significantly reduced prices.

INVESTMENT WEB SITES ON THE INTERNET

A plethora of personal finance Web sites have found their way into cyberspace in recent years. From background investment information for the novice, to online investment periodicals, to virtual brokerage accounts, to sophisticated investment research, to up-to-the-minute news that was formerly only available to investment professionals...it is now available to all of us with a click of the mouse. Moreover the amount of information and capabilities are expanding geometrically. The following sites, which are just a small but useful sampling of what is available, provide quite a bit of free information. Some have a charge for certain services, and many that do charge have a free trial period.

BASIC INVESTMENT INFORMATION

www.cboe.com – Chicago Board Options Exchange. This is the largest exchange for trading options. The CBOE Web site is a tremendously valuable resource about how options work. This is probably the best educational site about options available to the nonprofessional. The booklet *Characteristics and Risks of Standardized Options* is available on this Web site.

www.motleyfool.com – The Motley Fool. The real purpose of this Web site is to educate beginning investors in a certain approach to selecting stock purchases. The "Fool" motif, which runs throughout, keeps things fun and light, but the advice is serious and worthwhile. This organization is respected throughout the online world. Their approaches to investing, as well as the updated investment information each day, is well worth a look on an ongoing basis.

SUBSCRIPTION INVESTMENT SERVICES

www.valueline.com - Value Line Investment Survey (800-634-3583). This subscription service provides one-page summaries on more than 1,700 common stocks. The report on each stock has a "timeliness" and "safety" ranking from "1" to "5." Also included is a chart of the stock and financial data for at least the past twelve years. It also describes the company's business, recent developments, beta (a measure of the stock's volatility), and future expectations for the company. Prior to each section is an industry analysis describing the current situation, trends, and composite statistics for that industry. Service is also available in hard copy format.

ww.zacks.com – Zacks Investment Research (800-767-3771). There is a wealth of information on this site, both for free and for a charge. In addition to current quotes, statistics, an earnings calendar and news, there is a place to point and click to get the "Brokerage Firm Buy List" at no charge. For those who want the complete advisory service, sign up for the free trial by going to **www.zacksadvisor.com**. Service is also available in hard copy format.

DISCOUNT BROKERAGES

All of the following provide quotes on various securities and online investment capabilities for stocks, options, Exchange Traded Funds, bonds, mutual funds, and other types of investments. Some provide general business news, company specific news, investment research, and other information. This list is not meant to be exhaustive, but is representative of the largest online discount brokers. Information on these and other companies is available at libraries for non-computer users.

www.fidelity.com - Fidelity Investments; 800-544-5555

www.schwab.com - Charles Schwab & Co.; 800-2-SCHWAB

www.accutrade.com - Accutrade; 800-494-8939

www.ameritrade.com - Ameritrade; 800-454-9272

www.harrisdirect.com - Harris Direct; 800-825-5723

www.etrade.com - E-Trade; 800-ETRADE1

www.scottrade.com – Scottrade; 800-619-SAVE

www.tdwaterhouse.com - TD Waterhouse; 800-TDWATERHOUSE

PERIODICALS

www.barrons.com - *Barron's.* The Web site and weekly publication have articles on business and economic topics, individual industries and companies, stock market indicators and interviews with investment professionals. It also has regular sections on capital markets (including information on interest rate trends), real estate markets, international markets, commodities, and options. *Barron's* is known for its extensive statistics and quotations on different markets, indexes, and economic and investment indicators. Corporate earnings and dividends are reported as well.

www.businessweek.com - *Business Week.* The Web site and weekly magazine have various articles divided into sections such as current business and company news, international, economic analysis, government, people, labor, finance, information processing, science and technology, marketing, environment, and personal business. Specific investment ideas and recommendations usually are provided in the finance and personal business sections. Each issue features a cover article that addresses a major business, economic, or news subject. Economic and monetary indicators, economic trends, business outlook, and various investment data also are provided.

www.forbes.com – *Forbes.* The Web site and magazine contain a variety of articles divided into sections about companies, industries, government, international, taxes, investing, marketing, computers/communications, personal affairs, and careers. It also provides economic news and investment information and advice from different columnists.

www.fortune.com - *Fortune*. The Web site and magazine also consist of articles divided by sections on topics such as companies to watch, money and markets, selling, the environment, managing, the economy, innovation, and corporate performance. Articles on specific industries are common. Regular features include economic forecasts, news and trends, and personal investing, which provides specific investment recommendations and interviews with professional money managers. *Fortune* also devotes a special issue to investment ideas and recommendations.

www.investors.com – *Investor's Business Daily*. The Web site and daily newspaper contain quotations each business day for stocks, bonds, international currencies, options, futures, mutual funds, and foreign stocks. Charts for selected stocks, as well as major market indicators, are printed. There are also articles on certain companies, industries, and the U.S. economy. Earnings and dividend reports are presented.

www.money.com – *Money*. The Web site and magazine contain personal finance articles, some of which are investment oriented and some of which are consumer oriented. The articles cover a variety of investment vehicles and investment strategies. Specific investment recommendations are common. The articles are easy to read and are perhaps better for the relative novice.

www.wsj.com – *The Wall Street Journal*. The Web site and daily newspaper provide a wealth of information to the investor. They report various economic data as well as opinions from economists about their expectations for the economy. They also present articles on investment topics, trends, and advice and reports on different industries and different companies. They also supply quotations on stocks, bonds, options, Exchange Traded Funds, futures contracts, mutual funds, and foreign stocks and currencies for each business day. Corporate earnings and dividends are also reported.

INVESTMENT NEWS SITES

www.bestcalls.com – This site maintains a calendar of upcoming conference calls, the quarterly ritual during which executives discuss with analysts the recent performance and future prospects for their companies, which often provides valuable insights. The conference calls available are searchable by name or stock ticker symbol. These conference calls are becoming more and more public as a result of new disclosure rules for companies. Investors can sit in on the meetings via telephone or streaming audio links on the Web site. Recent calls are archived on the bestcalls.com site for ninety days.

www.briefing.com – Professional quality analysis of investment news. This is one of the most respected sources of daily stock market news online. The "Short Stories" feature describes individual companies making news during the course of the business day. Information includes brokerage company evaluation changes, technical stock analysis, earnings estimates, and much more.

www.cbs.marketwatch.com – In addition to a great deal of investment news, this site offers stock tracking, charting, broker research, industry analysis, and much more.

www.cnbc.com – CNBC. This cable TV channel, and the Web site that goes with it, has become a phenomenon. Investors of all types from day traders to long-term investors tune in to the TV show for hours daily to glean stock tips from guest analysts and portfolio managers in addition to feeling part of the CNBC "family" of regular commentators. Soon you won't feel complete without your daily dose of Bill, Joe, Sue, Maria, Bob, David, Michelle and all the rest. The brief talks live on the floor of The New York Stock Exchange with Art Cashin are a highlight as well as highly informative and humorous. The Web site mirrors all that is happening on the TV show, with up to date market news and also the stock pickers' selections. In addition, the site offers research capabilities, financial calculators, tax, retirement and other personal financial advice, career management links to other sites and message boards where CNBC community groupies can chat about their favorite stocks to love or hate. CNBC is owned by General Electric.

www.cnnfn.com – CNN Financial Network. Headlines, stories, and feature articles on hot business topics. CNN is owned by AOL/Time Warner.

OTHER SITES

www.10kwizard.com – If you are looking for company specific information beyond just financials and news, this is the site for you. 10K Wizard allows you to do a complete background check on a company by retrieving the quarterly and annual reports which publicly held companies are required to file with the Securities and Exchange Commission's EDGAR database. You can search for documents by company name, ticker symbol or a keyword. By registering at the site, it will send you an e-mail any time one of the companies you select files a report. This is heavy-duty information…and all of it is free.

www.amex.com - Web site of the American Stock Exchange. Among other things, the site contains a list of all Exchange Traded Funds (ETFs) which are available through that exchange.

www.bigcharts.com – Free charts, quotes, reports and indicators on over 50,000 stocks, mutual funds and indexes. The site lets you alter a graph's look with nine different designs from mountain and bar chart to candlestick and logarithmic.

www.google.com - Arguably the best search engine on the Internet. Type in whatever your are seeking to find information on and Google will likely lead you to many, many of the best Web sites that can find it.

CHECKING YOUR UNDERSTANDING: AN OPEN BOOK QUIZ

True or False:

_____ 1. Covered call options can be written on stocks an investor currently owns, or an investor can buy stocks with the specific intent of writing calls on them.

_____ 2. Stock trades cost more than option trades.

_____ 3. Writers of covered call options tend to have more stable investment returns than an investor who only buys and holds common stocks.

_____ 4. Premiums received from writing covered call options must be retained as cash in the investor's account until the option expiration date.

_____ 5. An option buyer is obligated to buy the stock covered by the option if the market price of the stock is greater than the strike price on expiration.

_____ 7. If the owner of stock writes an out-of-the-money call on his shares and the market price exceeds the strike price on expiration, the writer will receive a gain on his stock above its value at the time the option was written in addition to the premium income he received when the option transaction was initiated.

_____ 8. The expiration date for calls occurs at the end of the contract month.

_____ 9. The strike price is the price at which the option buyer has the right to purchase the shares subject to his option at any time up to and including the expiration date of the option.

_____ 10. Shares of JJJ Company are trading at $86 ¾. If options were written on the shares at a strike price of $90, the options would be considered to be in-the-money.

_____ 11. A person who owns stock and has options contracts written on it during a market decline in the stock will always be better off financially than a person who simply owns the stock during such a market decline and does not have options written on it.

_____ 12. AAA stock is selling at $28 per share. Earlier the owner of AAA shares had sold calls on his stock at a $25 strike price. If the current price of the calls is $4, then the intrinsic value of the option contracts is $1 and the time value of the contracts is $3

_____ 13. Writing call options is considered to be a conservative, more predictable investment strategy, whereas buying call options is considered to be a high risk strategy.

_____ 14. The reason that the passage of time is a friend of the covered call option writer is because the time value of a call declines toward zero as the option expiration date approaches.

_____ 15. Unlike many other investments, the writer of a covered call option receives cash on the day after the investment is made.

_____ 16. The time value of a call option is that part of the current option price that is considered to be attributable to the time remaining between now and the expiration date of the option contract.

_____ 17. LEAPS have expiration dates much longer than regular options, and therefore the option premiums will be greater.

_____ 18. An option writer can only buy back the option to close his position if the current market price is less than the price when the investor initially sold the options to open.

_____ 19. An investor pays commissions on options transactions when they are sold to open and also when they expire on the option expiration date.

_____ 20. Each option contract covers 100 shares of the underlying security.

_____ 21. When an investor writes covered call options, the buyer of the calls is entitled to any dividends paid during the term of the option contract.

_____ 22. For a stock or an option, the "bid" is the price at which a buyer is willing to purchase and the "ask" is the price at which a seller is willing to sell.

_____ 23. A call option on a stock with a beta of .8 would likely trade at a higher premium than a call option on a stock with a beta of 1.5, since a beta of .8 means greater volatility than a beta of 1.5.

_____ 24. Buyers of stock on margin have better returns with less risk because the opportunity for gain is greater than the margin interest cost.

_____ 25. Option writers should almost always place a limit order on trades rather than a market order due to the lower liquidity of options when compared with stocks and the wide spread that often exists between the bid and ask prices of options.

_____ 26. For a call option writer, the premium income received is taxed as a short-term capital gain at the time the premium income is received.

_____ 27. Writing covered calls on stocks in an IRA account can be attractive, since above average returns can potentially be achieved with no immediate income tax consequence.

_____ 28. Typically economists and institutional investors have been successful in timing the right points to enter and exit the stock market.

_____ 29. Markets usually go down before a decline in economic activity.

_____ 30. Markets usually go up before or at the beginning of an economic recovery.

Multiple Choice:

31. To turn a $100,000 investment into $1 million over a twenty-year time period, an investor would need to obtain a compounded annual return of
a. just over 6%
b. about 8%
c. just over 12%
d. about 20%

32. The above normal returns realized by investors in stocks during the decade of the 1990s, the "dot com" bubble, and excesses in capital investment will likely mean the stock market returns in the future
a. should remain equally strong
b. should be even greater
c. may likely be significantly less
d. will always be subject to wild volatility

33. A conservative investor with $50,000 in investment funds who wishes to use options to increase his total investment return might consider
a. buying Exchange Traded Funds and writing covered calls on the shares.

b. buying an individual stock and writing covered calls on the shares

c. buying calls on an Exchange Traded Fund in anticipation of price appreciation

d. buying calls on a stock in anticipation of price appreciation

34. Investment diversification can be fostered by

a. owning a group of twenty or more common stocks representing a broad range of industries

b. purchase of shares in Exchange Traded Funds rather than just owning one individual stock

c. balancing a portfolio between cash, fixed income securities and stocks

d. all of the above

35. The worst case scenario for a covered call option writer would be if

a. the price of the stock exceeds the strike price on expiration

b. the buyer of the option does not exercise the option at expiration

c. the market price of the stock declines by more than the call option premium received

d. the call option is bought to close prior to expiration at a lower price than it was sold to open

36. To determine whether a potential option writing opportunity meets an investor's goal, the investor should give the strongest consideration to

a. option premium and dividend income

b. dividend income and capital appreciation

c. option premium and capital appreciation

d. option premium, dividend income and capital appreciation

37. Investors should generally write out-of-the-money covered calls unless
a. a market decline is anticipated
b. a market rise is anticipated
c. a flat market environment is anticipated
d. the investor is unsure of where the market is headed

38. If an investor buys and holds a call and, on expiration, the strike price is greater than the price of the underlying stock, the investor
a. will have a gain
b. will have a partial loss
c. will lose his entire investment
d. will break even

39. For an option writer, the most desirable outcome on the expiration date would be if
a. the price of the underlying stock is well below the strike price
b. the option is significantly in-the-money
c. the decline in the price of the underlying stock is offset by the option premium
d. the price of the underlying stock is just slightly below the strike price

40. The largest premium will be received by writing covered calls if
a. the stock price is the same as the strike price and the expiration date is one month away.

b. the stock price is below the strike price and the expiration date is one month away.

c. the stock price is the same as the strike price and the expiration date is three months away.

d. the stock price is below the strike price and the expiration date is three months away.

41. Warren has 1,000 shares of JJJ valued at $60,000. He writes 10 call contracts to expire in July at $5 ½ per contract and takes no further action. At expiration Warren retains his stock, which is then valued at $58,000. How much ahead during this time period is Joe compared to another shareholder with 1,000 shares of JJJ who simply held the shares and did not write options?

a. $2,000

b. $3,500

c. $5,500

d. no difference

42. Warren owned 1,000 shares of AAA Company. He wrote 10 calls to open at a premium of $4 per contract. The market declined in his shares, and accordingly the price of the options declined as well. Warren bought the 10 calls to close at $1.50. The result of these option transactions for Joe was

a. a loss of $4,000

b. a loss of $2,500

c. a gain of $2,500

d. no gain or loss

43. Writing call options on stock you own is considered to be a conservative strategy because

a. there is more predictability to investment returns

b. writing stock options provides downside protection in the event of a market downturn

c. the writer of the option receives a fixed premium income in advance as a tradeoff for the possibility of substantial short-term price appreciation in the stock.

d. all of the above

44. Writing call options on stock you own is a strategy that works best when the stock markets are

a. rapidly rising

b. declining precipitously

c. flat or rising somewhat

d. outperforming bonds and CDs

45. Option premiums would likely be higher for call options on a stock that is

a. less volatile

b. more volatile

c. a utility stock rather than a technology stock

d. underperforming the market

46. You buy 2,000 shares of BBB at $18 per share and immediately write 10 call contracts at a strike price of $20 on half of your stock position. The price you receive on the calls is $2 per contract. On expiration the price of the stock is $21. How much gain have you realized on the shares subject to the calls compared to the shares that were not subject to the calls?

a. The gain on the shares subject to the calls was the same as the shares not subject to the calls.

b. The gain on the shares subject to the calls was $1,000 greater than the shares not subject to the calls.

c. The gain on the shares not subject to the calls was $1,000 greater than the shares subject to the calls.
d. The gain on the shares not subject to the calls was $3,000 greater than the shares subject to the calls.

47. If you owned shares of XXX Company currently valued at $100 per share, you would receive the highest premium if you would write call contracts
a. where the strike price was substantially higher than $100
b. with a strike price of $110
c. with a strike price of $105
d. at least $10 out-of-the-money

48. Joe sold call options on his stock at a strike price of $60. The stock is currently trading at $58 ½ and the option is trading at $3. Regarding the options he has written, at the current price of $3
a. $1 ½ of the premium is intrinsic value and $1 ½ is time value
b. $1 of the premium is intrinsic value and $2 is time value
c. all $3 of the premium is intrinsic value
d. all $3 of the premium is time value

49. In a steadily declining stock market
a. the total return if options have been written on stocks will be worse than just owning stocks on which no options have been written
b. the total return if options have been written on stocks will be better than just owning stocks on which no options have been written

c. there is essentially no difference in the performance of stocks on which options have been written and stocks on which options have not been written in a declining market
d. buying calls would yield the greatest return

50. For a call option writer, the most profitable situation would occur if
a. the market price of the underlying stock is just above the strike price when the option expires
b. the price of the stock remains the same at expiration as it was when the option transaction was initiated
c. the call expires worthless
d. the price of the stock is lower than the strike price and the market price of the underlying stock when the option transaction was initiated

51. The purpose of diversification in investments is to
a. assure the maximum possible return
b. reduce risk
c. assure a good return when writing covered calls on the underlying securities
d. none of the above

52. An investor looking at option writing opportunities on a stock would generally find that
a. LEAPS provide the best annualized yield
b. Shorter-term options provide the highest premium income
c. LEAPS provide higher premium income than shorter-term options but a lower annualized yield
d. A six month option would offer the highest premium and yield

53. Actions taken by the Federal Reserve Bank can have an impact on economic activity when the Fed
a. raises or lowers short-term interest rates
b. increases or reduces the money supply
c. both a and b
d. neither a or b

54. Warren owns 1,000 shares of YYY common stock. He has considered writing covered call option contracts on this stock. It was purchased ten years ago at $1.50 per share. Its current market value is $80 per share. He believes that the stock will remain fairly flat or only increase nominally in value over the next six months due to economic conditions and his assessment of the company's near-term earnings prospects. If Warren's beliefs about the economy and the prospects for YYY stock are correct, it would probably be best for Warren to
a. Write in-the-money calls for maximum downside protection
b. Write calls that are enough out-of-the-money to obtain some premium income but not trigger the capital gain tax.
c. Sell the stock and pay the capital gain tax
d. Retain the stock but not write call options on it

55. Warren has been doing an assessment of current economic conditions. The yield curve is positive. The Fed has been reducing interest rates, but probably won't reduce them further. Capital spending seems to have been increasing and unemployment has been declining slightly. If Warren's assessment of the economy is correct, his call option writing strategy should probably be to

a. Stop writing options on his stocks for the next few months until stock prices have moved up significantly.
b. Write in-the-money calls for maximum downside protection.
c. Sell his financial stocks, as interest rates are unlikely to decline further.
d. Write out-of-the-money calls to receive premium income, leaving some room for additional capital appreciation.

ANSWER KEY TO QUIZ

1.   T   Both work equally well.
2.   F   Option trades usually cost more than the trade for stock.
3.   T   The premium income stabilizes the return.
4.   F   The premium can be withdrawn or invested.
5.   F   The option buyer is not obligated to do anything.
6.   T   Up front is much better than later, don't you think?
7.   T   The highest overall return for an option writer.
8.   F   The Saturday following the third Friday of each month.
9.   T   The right, but not the obligation.
10.   F   They are out-of-the-money.
11.   T   The premium provides some price protection.
12.   F   The intrinsic value is $3 and the time value is $1.
13.   T   Aren't you glad you are a seller of options and not a buyer?
14.   T   Time is an option writer's best friend!
15.   T   What other investment pays you cash up front?
16.   T   The time value of options will be a major source of income for you.
17.   T   But the total yield will be lower.
18.   F   The position can be closed out at any time and at any price.
19.   F   There is no commission paid when options expire worthless.
20.   T   This is true for options on all stocks and Exchange

Traded Funds.

21. F   As a writer of calls, you still own the stock and get the dividends.

22. T   To write covered calls, you will seek a price about in the middle.

23. F   The exact opposite is true.

24. F   That may be true at times, but it is certainly not always true.

25. T   You should almost always protect yourself with a limit price.

26. F   The premium income is taxed as of the date the option expires.

27. T   No income tax to pay until funds are withdrawn from an IRA.

28. F   Almost no one has this ability on an ongoing basis.

29. T   That's why it is so hard to pick exit points.

30. T   That's why it is so hard to pick entry points.

31. C   Refer back to the chart in the Preface.

32. C   The opinion of Warren Buffett and many other wise investors.

33. A   Diversification can easily be obtained through ETFs.

34. D   There are many different facets of diversification.

35. C   This is the only time an option writer experiences an actual loss.

36. A   Capital appreciation may occur, but you can't count on it.

37. A   In a market decline, in-the-money calls provide the most protection.

38. C   Again, aren't you glad you're the seller and not the buyer?

39. D   Next time you can get either more premium or a

higher strike price.

40. C Stock price, strike price and time to expiration all play a role.

41. B $5,500 in premium income, less a $2,000 decline in stock price.

42. C 1,000 x 4 = $4,000, less 1,000 x $1.50 = a $2,500 gain.

43. D There are a lot of advantages to writing covered calls.

44. C Doesn't that sound like what Warren Buffett is predicting?

45. B So, a higher premium for options on AOL than on Exxon Mobil.

46. B 1,000 x $2 = $2,000 + $2,000 gain = $4,000 vs. a $3,000 gain.

47. C A closer strike price to the market price means a greater premium.

48. D It's all time value when market price is below the strike price.

49. B Again, there is downside protection "insurance."

50. A Your stock is sold and you have achieved your maximum return.

51. B Always an important investment consideration.

52. C That's how it works.

53. C Watching trends in short-term rates and the money supply can tell you a lot about the future economy.

54. B He can always roll forward or roll up if the stock goes up in value.

55. D This is a pretty good environment for normal call writing activity.

INDEX

TIME IS YOUR BEST FRIEND...
NOT JUST WHEN WRITING
COVERED CALLS,
BUT IN LIFE!

* * * * * * * *

If you had a bank that put $86,400 into your account each morning, allowed you to keep no cash in your account at the end of 24 hours and canceled out whatever part of that amount you failed to use, what would you do? Try to spend every cent, of course!

Well, everyone does have such a bank, and its name is **TIME**. Every morning it credits you with 86,400 seconds. The next morning, at the same hour, you have lost whatever amount of it you failed to invest in good purposes. It carries over no balance and allows no overdrafts. If you don't use the day's deposit, the loss is yours. There is no going back and no drawing in advance against tomorrow.

How do you spend your daily surplus? Best wishes for an enormous return on your investment...today!

Unknown

ABOUT THE AUTHOR

As a thirty-year career banker and trust officer for Norwest Corporation, now Wells Fargo & Co., one of the nation's largest financial institutions, Paul D. Kadavy was president of numerous banks in three states. He also headed a multi-billion dollar trust department, managed a team of investment professionals, and was a trusted advisor to many of the banks' individual clients. He is now retired from banking and is a writer, teacher and public speaker.

Kadavy has served as a faculty member of the National Graduate Trust School at Northwestern University, The Schools of Banking, Inc., the American Institute of Banking and numerous community colleges in several states. He has been a lecturer on trust, investment and banking subjects to FDIC and Federal Reserve Bank examiners in Washington, D.C. He has been a public speaker for the past twenty-five years.

Kadavy is also the author of *Covered Call Writing With Exchange Traded Funds (ETFs)* (ISBN 0-9715514-2-1), *Covered Call Writing With Qs And Diamonds* (ISBN 0-9715514-3-X), and *The Book of World-Class Quotations: The Best of the Best Quotations on Earth* (ISBN 0-9715514-1-3), which includes guides for writing affirmations and for personal goal setting. All of his books are available through Amazon.com and Arrow Publications (www.arrowpublications.net). In addition to writing books, he is the author of banking, trust and investment articles for such national publications as *Financial Review*, *Trusts & Estates*, *Pension World*, *The Collector/Investor*, *Cases & Comment* and *American Bankers Association Trust Management*.

He has developed and successfully used the principles in books for over twenty years.

MANUAL WORKSHEET FOR COVERED CALL OPTION WRITING OPPORTUNITIES

(A) Company	(B) Symbol	(C) # of Shares	(D) Share Price	(E) Market Value	(F) Div.	(G) Option Expir.	(H) Strike	(I) Days	(J) Option Symbol	(K) Prem.	(L) Prem. Inc.	(M) Prem. $ Per Day	(N) Contract Yield	(O) Total Annual Yield	(P) Max. Cap. Gain	(Q) Annual Yield/W Cap. Gain

MANUAL WORKSHEET FOR COVERED CALL OPTION WRITING OPPORTUNITIES

(A) Company	(B) Symbol	(C) # of Shares	(D) Share Price	(E) Market Value	(F) Div.	(G) Option Expir.	(H) Strike	(I) Days	(J) Option Symbol	(K) Prem.	(L) Prem. Inc.	(M) Prem. $ Per Day	(N) Contract Yield	(O) Total Annual Yield	(P) Max. Cap. Gain	(Q) Annual Yield/W Cap. Gain

MANUAL WORKSHEET FOR TRACKING OPTION WRITING **TRANSACTIONS**

(A) Company	(B) Symbol	(C) # of Shares	(D) Share Price	(E) Market Value	(F) Trade Date	(G) Option Expir.	(H) Strike	(I) Days	(J) Option Symbol	(K) Prem.	(L) Prem. Inc.	(M) Stock Gain/Loss	(N) Total Dollar Return	(O) Annual Percentage Return

MANUAL WORKSHEET FOR TRACKING OPTION WRITING TRANSACTIONS

(A)	(B)	(C)	(D)	(E)	(F)	(G)	(H)	(I)	(J)	(K)	(L)	(M)	(N)	(O)
Company	Symbol	# of Shares	Share Price	Market Value	Trade Date	Option Expir.	Strike	Days	Option Symbol	Prem.	Prem. Inc.	Stock Gain/Loss	Total Dollar Return	Annual Percentage Return